The Trial of Phillis Wheatley

A Play in Two Acts

By

Ronald B. Wheatley

ISBN: 1481966189
ISBN 13: 9781481966184
Library of Congress Control Number: 2013917130
CreateSpace Independent Publishing Platform
North Charleston, South Carolina

For Ethel

And

In memory of Matthew Striggles

DRAMATIS PERSONAE

Phillis Wheatley
Mary Wheatley
Susannah Wheatley
John Wheatley
Nathaniel Wheatley
Gov. Thomas Hutchinson
Lt. Gov. Andrew Oliver
Rev. Samuel Cooper
Joseph Green, Esq.
Rev. Charles Chauncy
Hon. Thomas Hubbard
Hon. James Bowdoin
Rev. Samuel Mather
Rev. Mather Byles
Hon. John Erving
Rev. Andrew Elliot
Hon. Harrison Gray
John Hancock, Esq
Ebenezer Mackintosh
Samuel Swift
Ensemble

MAIN ENTRANCE

The Trial of Phillis Wheatley

Written by Ronald B. Wheatley

Directed by Stephen Levine

Costume Design
Jessica Banks

Set Design

Light Design
Stephen Levine,
Noreen White, &
Arthur Sharpe

Stage Manager
Jessica Davis

ARTISTIC AND PRODUCTION STAFF

In Celebration of

BLACK HISTORY month

Save the date!

The Trial of Phillis Wheatley

WORLD PREMIERE

Friday, Feb. 7th, 2003
Saturday, Feb. 8th, 2003
8:00pm

A NOTE FROM THE DIRECTOR

The Trial of Phillis Wheatley

The Trial of Phillis Wheatley

A Note from the Director

On first reading Ron Wheatley's play, *The Trial Of Phillis Wheatley*, its literary and theatrical potential were dazzling to me as a theater professor and theater director. Having some familiarity with Phillis Wheatley's Revolutionary War era poetry, I was immediately impressed with the fascinating historical truth underlying the play that demanded literary attention. Especially significant was the structural climax of the play when all the leaders of the Province Massachusetts Bay Colony, including John Hancock, signed a document attesting to the authorship of an African-American slave as the most famous child prodigy-poet in the Colonies, Phillis Wheatley. In the play, Ron Wheatley brilliantly connects this signed document to a prior attestation signed by a group of American patriots who formed a protest group in opposition to the British Parliament's passage and imposition of the Stamp Act on Boston – that group chose the name "The Sons of Liberty." These two historical documents are now seen as important precursors of The Declaration of Independence, the most important American Revolution document of all, ultimately signed by some of the same men.

Anyone whose life-long career is teaching theater, including me, has a secret fantasy: having the chance to cast all of the best students over so many years in one play! The Trial of Philiis Wheatley presented me such an opportunity.

The play also appealed to me as a theatrical director, as it emerged as a wonderful opportunity to unite the entire

Bridgewater college-university-town community during Black History Month. Because so many of the jury characters in this play are older men, roles not best suited to young college students, they presented another unusual opportunity. Those jury characters could be played perfectly by faculty, administrators, and alumni, led by then Massachusetts State Representative Peter Koutoujian, who was outstanding as John Hancock! And Phillis Wheatley was played by Shannon Stanton, a student whose father and grandmother I had directed on the same stage!

I can never thank Ron Wheatley enough for writing *The Trial of Phillis Wheatley*, and the entire Bridgewater State University and community are proud to have produced such an outstanding stage success.

Stephen Levine
April 25, 2013

Acknowledgements

There are so many people to thank in the production of a stage play that it is impossible to name everyone involved, so I can only skim the surface. Toward that end I have inserted at the front a copy of the poster promoting the play that includes the program of the first performance of "The Trial of Phillis Wheatley," at the Horace Mann Theater on February 7, 2003.

The actors deserve special mention for their hard work, and enthusiasm in the production, as do those unsung heroes of the theater who work their magic with stagecraft, sound and lighting.

I would like to thank playwright and screenwriter John Guare, who read an early draft version and provided comments, and playwright Kuros Charney who reviewed a later version and provided suggestions.

Every produced play needs a champion, and Matthew Striggles, now deceased, served that purpose. I want to make a special recognition to him and his wife, Gloria, who supported the idea from the beginning.

Of course, direction is key, and no one deserves more credit than Stephen Levine who at the time of the first production was a member of the faculty at Bridgewater State College in Bridgewater, Massachusetts. My goal in the play was to try to bring Phillis to life, and Stephen did that brilliantly. I would be remiss by not acknowledging his former wife, Sharon Waters, who served a dual role in participating in early readings around the dinner table with Stephen and my wife, Ethel, and me, and who played so well the role of Susanna Wheatley in the performances.

A special thanks to my dear and glorious physician friend, Dr. Michael Johnson, of Scituate, and Owen O'Malley, of Cohasset, retired teacher at the Latin School in Boston, and fellow colleague in the Massachusetts Bar Association. Both men share my interest in the history of the place and time, and both labored over the manuscript checking details, correcting grammar, spelling and typos, and general editing. However, I am responsible for any mistakes that remain.

Finally the play could not have been produced as it was without the cooperation of Bridgewater State College, (now Bridgewater State University.)

If I have left anyone out, it was unintentional and I apologize.

Time-line of key events

ca. 1753 - A female child prodigy is born in West Africa, some scholars say in Senegal, others say Gambia, but it could be anywhere along what was known as "The windward coast," (mainly from Senegal to Nigeria, but extending down to the Congo).

ca. 1758-1760 - That child prodigy is captured by slavers probably with her mother and father, if so, they are soon separated.

1760 - In November the newly constructed brig *Phillis* sets sail from Boston Harbor on her maiden voyage with a cargo designed for trading slaves along the windward coast. Her captain, Peter Gwynn, carries letters from the ship's owner, Timothy Fitch, Boston's most notorious slave trader, to take up to 70 slaves and "to be sure to bring as few women and girls as possible."

ca. April-May-June 1761 somewhere along the "windward coast" where the child prodigy is held in a "factory" (a slave holding pen) she is taken on board the brig *Phillis* and soon thereafter endures the ordeals of the "middle passage."

July 1761 - the *Phillis* arrives at Beach Street wharf (now Chinatown) in Boston carrying approximately 75 human cargo. Boston slave storeowner John Avery puts out an advertisement in local papers that "in the parcel" were "several small Negroes."

July 12, 1761 - Susanna Wheatley, a devout Christian and member of the Old South Church congregation in Boston rescues by purchase the approximately seven-year-old child prodigy from the *Phillis* and takes her home to the Wheatley mansion less than a mile away. The Wheatley family, John and Susanna and their teenage twins, Mary and Nathaniel, name the child Phillis after the brig that brought her.

July 1761-November 1772 - the time of the play, the Wheatley family raise Phillis as a member of the family in the Wheatley mansion located at the corner of King's Street and Mackerel Lane, (now the intersection of Kilby and State Street). The Wheatley family designated their 18-year old-daughter, Mary, twin sister of Nathaniel, to take on the job of tutoring Phillis. Within 18 months Phillis is reading and understanding even the more difficult passages in the Bible. Susanna Wheatley becomes America's first stage mother promoting Phillis' amazing writing accomplishments. While some northern colonial slave owners taught their "servants" to read so they could read the Bible and become Christians, the level of education provided to Phillis by the Wheatley family could be said to have been unprecedented.

1761- Boston Attorney James Otis representing Boston merchants challenges the renewal of the Writs of Assistance that had been introduced a decade earlier as part of the British Empire rules of Trade. The renewal allowed custom inspectors to conduct warrantless searches and seizures on Boston businesses and private homes.

1765 - British Parliament passed the Stamp Act requiring that many printed materials in the colonies be produced on paper with a special stamp imported from London. Such special paper was necessary under the law for the preparation of legal documents, magazines, newspapers and many other types of printed materials used throughout the colonies. The purpose of the tax was to help pay costs for administration of the colonies including payment for troops stationed in North America following the French and Indian War, or Seven Years War.

1765 – 1770 - During this half a decade an organized mob, taking direction from a secret policy making group calling themselves the Loyal Nine, ruled the streets of Boston intimidating merchants and Tories for political ends.

1765 – Phillis Wheatley composes her first poem.

1767 – The Townsend Revenue Act is passed by Parliament to raise money through taxes on glass, paint, lead, and paper for the British administration of certain colonies in North America. This renewed the still simmering hostility to the Stamp Act.

1767 – Phillis Wheatley's first poem is published at the age of 14.

1768 - A secret society is formed in Boston naming itself the "Sons of Liberty" in opposition to the Stamp Act. On August 28, 1768 the members of the Sons of Liberty sign their Attestation at a picnic in Dorchester. This group would soon evolve into the Tea Party Movement.

1768 - Customs officials seize John Hancock's sloop the *Liberty* in Boston Harbor for "smuggling" which in turn led Bostonians to raid the Custom House.

1768 - British troops occupy Boston on October 1, 1768 meeting little resistance. Rather, Bostonians changed tactics to establish the Non-Importation agreements that spread to other colonies resulting in huge losses to British trade.

1770 - the Boston Massacre occurred on March 5, 1770, when a group of Bostonians gathered after a confrontation at a British guard post. It resulted in the death of five citizens of Boston, one a teenager. The seemingly spontaneous eruption was the result of the culmination of tensions in Boston that had been growing since Royal troops first appeared on October 1, 1768 to enforce the tax burden imposed by the Townshend Acts. It occurred just adjacent to the Wheatley mansion.

1770 - Phillis receives international acclaim for her elegy on Reverend George Whitefield, a charismatic British preacher who died in September 1770, while on a tour of New England that included speaking from the pulpit at the Old South Meeting House. Phillis heard him preach his message of the "New Awakening" urging love of fellow man, and reaching out to the poor, the orphans, widows, and those held in bondage as slaves. The Countess of Huntingdon in England upon reading Phillis Wheatley's elegy on George Whitefield was so impressed she becomes an important patron of Phillis in England. By 1770 Phillis had composed enough poems to consider having them published in a volume.

1771-1774 - Thomas Hutchinson served as governor of Massachusetts Bay Colony. He had been Lieutenant Governor prior to becoming governor. Against his wishes, he was also appointed Chief Justice by his predecessor. Although he was not unsympathetic to the grievances of the colonists, he opposed independence. He supported the Stamp Act publically, but infuriated the colonists by saying he opposed it privately. He justified this contradiction by his policy of defending British rule over the colonies. His pro-British policies became increasingly unpopular, contributing to growing unrest. In 1774, he was replaced by a military governor, British General Thomas Gage. To his credit, Hutchinson was a scholar, and historian who wrote what has been called the seminal history of Boston. In an irony of history, like his ancestor Ann Hutchinson, he died in exile in Britain estranged from his ancestral home - Boston.

1772 - In June Lord Mansfield (William Murray) Chief Justice of King's Bench, the highest Court in England, in the case ***Somerset v Stewart*** (1772) 98 ER 499, "helped launch the movements to abolish slavery in England and the United States,"[1] in a watershed decision declaring that slavery was not countenanced by the laws of England.

1772 - November - Phillis was summoned by Governor Hutchinson to the Governor's Council Chamber to appear before a jury of eighteen of the most prominent men in Boston to defend her claim that she is the true and sole author of her manuscript for a proposed book of her poems to be published in Boston.

1773 – Nathaniel Wheatley accompanies Phillis Wheatley on a voyage to London. There she meets many notables and arrangements are being made for her to meet the Royal family,

---

1 The African American experience Encyclopedia of Antislavery and Abolition. Page 1.

but her visit is cut short when she learns her mistress is very ill, and she sailed back to Boston.

1773 – Phillis Wheatley's manuscript of "Poems On Various Subjects, Religious and Moral" was published in England and reprinted four times in London.

1734 – 1775 – November 5 in Boston was commemorated as Pope Day or Pope's Day in Boston celebrating what was known as Guy Fawkes Day in England. On November 5, 1605, Guy Fawkes and other conspirators were caught trying to blow up Parliament with the intent of crowning a Catholic monarch. In Boston the day was an unofficial holiday for manual laborers and apprentices. It was an anti-Catholic themed event where revelers would carry and eventually burn effigies of the Pope and other symbols of the Catholic Church. Once the "festivities" got underway later in the day, there were often violent street confrontations. When George Washington took command of the Continental Army at his headquarters in Cambridge, he put out a general order forbidding his troops from participating in Pope's Day activities since many of his best soldiers were Irish and Catholic. That act spelled the end to the annual event.

Preface

November 1772 marks the beginning of the end of what has been labeled "the period of calm," an almost three-year time span between the breakup of the boycott in Massachusetts and other colonies of English goods, the non-importation agreement in the fall of 1770, and the Boston Tea Party in December 1773. With trade between America and England restored, a new era of prosperity was returning to the seaport cities such as Boston. During this period, Americans imported more goods from England than ever before.

On the political front, things were relatively quiet as well. There was a new spirit of cooperation between the patriots and those who would remain loyal to the King in the future. With the collapse of the trade embargo on British imports, political leaders during the earlier troubles turned from politics to commerce. John Hancock acquiesced in the use of his ships to bring tea from England.[2] John Adams's successful defense of the British soldiers who participated in the Boston Massacre was a mixed blessing for him. While demonstrating that even unpopular defendants could get a fair trial in America, John Adams suffered personal and business setbacks because of it. Fearing more controversy, he seemed to have retired from politics to focus on his law practice. James Otis, the Boston lawyer who so eloquently led the opposition to the draconian search

---

[2] Benjamin Woods Labaree, *The Boston Tea Party* (Boston: Northeastern University Press, 1964), 80; William M. Fowler, Jr., *The Baron of Beacon Hill* (Boston: Houghton Mifflin Company, 1980), "It is to his credit that in all of his vast business dealings there is no evidence to suggest that he [John Hancock] himself ever bought or sold this commodity [slaves]."

and seizure policy embodied in the Writs of Assistance of the last decade, had been felled by a Tory's blow to his head; his once brilliant mind was now subject to periods of delusion.

Indeed, during 1772, the Tories, including Governor Thomas Hutchinson, were pleased that there appeared to be a split at the leadership level of the Whigs between John Hancock and Sam Adams, because the former thought the latter at times overbearing and uncompromising.[3] In the spring of that year, Governor Hutchinson, sensing the possibility of rapprochement with Hancock, sent him a message that he would support Hancock's election to the Governor's Council. While Hancock declined, replying that he was retiring from politics, he did accept a commission from the governor to serve as colonel of the Corps of Cadets of the Massachusetts militia, headquartered in Boston. However, Hancock's supposed retirement was short-lived, for in May of that year, the elections in Boston returned Hancock as a representative to the General Court, the provincial House of Representatives.

Following those elections, the House of Representatives asked the governor to consent to returning their place of meeting to Boston. The governor's edict to remove the legislature's meeting place across the Charles River to Cambridge still rankled, and had been the subject of a bitter two-year dispute. In the spirit of compromise of the moment, the governor consented, easing temporarily two years of acrimony on that issue, and allowed the court to reconvene in Boston for its June meeting. "What followed was a wistful dalliance between the two [Hutchinson and Hancock]. Later, Hancock's enemies would charge that he [Hancock] had been taken in by

---

[3] William M. Fowler, Jr., *The Baron of Beacon Hill*, 78.

Hutchinson's wiles."[4] The startling news that the governor's salary was being paid directly from London—contrary to the declaration of the House that the governor was to receive his sole support from acts of the General Assembly—was confirmed in July, undermining this relatively tranquil period.

This confirmation was followed by the shocking announcement in the fall from the British Ministry that, like the salary of the governor, all payments to the judges in the colony would be paid directly by London. This second body blow stunned the Whigs, who were still reeling from the governor's salary being independent from the legislature. The Whigs realized that direct payments by London to the judges threatened to undermine the independence of the judiciary. At the same time, there was still resentment that the governor claimed, on behalf of the King, the power to move the location of the General Assembly on a whim.

Simmering just under the surface, and ready for action at a moment's notice, was the mob. As Hiller B. Zobel observes: "The value of Boston's mobbish tradition lay in the immediate availability of a corps of husky, willing bully-boys." From 1765 through the early 1770's, the Boston mob became a handy tool for intimidation for political ends. The absence of an organized and well-manned constabulary left the mob and its leaders a great deal of control over the small island-like city of Boston, now burgeoning with about fifteen thousand souls.

So it was in Boston on that stormy night in November 1772, when our play opens.

---

4 William M. Fowler, Jr., *The Baron of Beacon Hill*, 139; Hiller B. Zobel, *The Boston Massacre* (New York: W. W. Norton & Company, 1970), 26.

(In Order of Appearance)

Phillis Wheatley
Mary Wheatley
Susanna Wheatley
John Wheatley
Nathaniel Wheatley
Bailiff/Clerk of the Court
Governor Thomas Hutchinson
Lieutenant Governor Andrew Oliver
John Hancock, Esq.
The Honorable Thomas Hubbard
The Honorable John Erving
The Honorable James Pitts
The Honorable Harrison Gray
The Honorable James Bowdoin
Joseph Green, Esq.
Richard Carey
The Rev. Charles Chauncy, D.D.
The Rev. Mather Byles, D.D.
The Rev. Edward Pemberton, D.D.
The Rev. Andrew Elliot, D.D.
The Rev. Samuel Cooper, D.D.
The Rev. Samuel Mather, D.D.
The Rev. John Moorhead
Ebenezer Mackintosh

People in the Play in Their Historical Context

Phillis Wheatley: Approximately eighteen years old. She has the fine features of a member of the Fulani tribe from what is now the northern part of Nigeria, West Africa. Blessed with a brilliant mind, a flair for language, and the ambition to excel as a poet. She has support from the family she serves in pursuing this ambition. Small and on the frail side, recovering from consumption. She is the household slave of John and Susanna Wheatley.

Mary Wheatley: Late twenties. Daughter of John and Susanna Wheatley, twin sister of Nathaniel Wheatley; she is somewhat frail. A brilliant student, she is assigned the task by her parents to tutor Phillis. She is devoted to her family and to Phillis, whom she has tutored for the past ten or so years. Like other Wheatley family members she is a devout Christian. She is attractive and married to the Reverend John Lathrop of Boston.

Susanna Wheatley: Early-sixties, she is the wife of John Wheatley and mother of the surviving children, twins Mary and Nathaniel. She is a devout Christian and a member of the Old South Congregational Church. She is devoted to Phillis and particularly supportive of her efforts in writing poetry and a proud promoter of Phillis' work. She may be America's first stage mother.

John Wheatley: Sixty-nine, he is the patriarch of the Wheatley family, husband of Susanna Wheatley and father of Mary and Nathaniel. Socially prominent Boston tailor and merchant shipper, he owns his own ship, *the London Packet,* for trade with England. He is proud of his accomplishment that he has built the family fortune by his hard work and good fortune. He is conservative in politics and business and a staunch loyalist. He is of medium height and somewhat overweight.

Nathaniel Wheatley: Late twenties. He is the son of John and Susanna Wheatley; and twin brother of Mary Wheatley. He is thin, athletic, handsome; and a bachelor. He is involved in his father's business and heir apparent to take it over. Like his sister, he is devoted to his family and to Phillis. He has helped tutor her since she came to the family at the approximate age of seven. Unknown to his parents he has put his name to an attestation five years prior to the time of the play that he is a member of the Sons of Liberty.

Thomas Hutchinson: Early sixties, he is to be the last civilian governor of the Province of Massachusetts Bay Colony, and like his ancestor, Anne Hutchinson, who was exiled from Boston in the 1630s for her alleged heretical religious beliefs, to die in exile, he is destined to meet the same fate. From a wealthy trading family, the House of Hutchinson, he spent most of his life serving in various political offices from Boston's Board of Selectman (1737), to Member of the Legislature for a decade, to Lieutenant Governor, Chief justice of the

Supreme Judicial Court, (even though not trained to the law or a member of the Boston Bar) and finally Governor. Tall and imperially slim, distinguished-looking. He was filled with a sense of his own superior judgment. He was a staunch loyalist, convinced that those organized in opposition to the King's policies in New England were in error. Agreeing to serve, although reluctantly, in the dual capacity of Governor and Chief Justice earned him the undying enmity of two powerful advocates of independence, James Otis, Jr. and Sam Adams. Hutchinson supported the Stamp Act publically, but said he opposed it privately. At the time of the play he was still optimistic that a break with the mother country could be avoided and the factions reconciled.

Andrew Oliver: Late sixties, he was destined to be the last civilian lieutenant governor of Massachusetts Bay Colony. He was the brother-in-law of Thomas Hutchinson and he had served as commissioner of customs prior to becoming Lieutenant Governor. At the time of the play he has not fully recovered from being hung in effigy on the Liberty Tree and having his house burned by the mob during the Stamp Act controversy of the past decade. Following the leadership of his brother-in-law, the governor, with whom he has cast his lot, he desperately wants to return the colony to the King and share in the rewards for this feat. In the play he acts as prosecutor.

John Hancock: Mid-thirties. He is on the small side and slight of build but athletic and handsome. Wears a forest green silk suit, in contrast to the black and dark gray woolen suits of the rest of the male cast. He is a prominent Boston merchant engaged in international trade and committed to public service, and has a distinguished record of public service, as member of the Boston Board of Selectman and in the legislature. He is heir to his uncle Thomas's business and fortune. By some accounts he is the wealthiest man in New England. Articulate, ambitious, and active in civic affairs, he has a flair for the dramatic and can be a mesmerizing public speaker. In the play he acts as the defense attorney. He is perceived by the Tories as one of the more reasonable members of the Whigs' leadership.

The Honorable Thomas Hubbard: seventy-one, member of the jury.[5] He was born in Boston, graduated from Harvard College and went on to serve as Treasurer of Harvard University from 1752 to 1773. He also served as Commissary General of the Province of Massachusetts Bay from 1759 to 1771. He was a successful businessman and investor who made land purchases in Maine and on the western frontier of the New England colonies. Hubbard was active in civic and religious affairs in Boston throughout his adult life. He served as a deacon of Old South Church for twenty-five years. He acted as an organizer for the Massachusetts Society for Propagating Christian Knowledge among the Indians of North

[5] James A. Levemier and Douglas R. Wilmes, eds., *American Writers Before 1800: A Biographical and Critical Dictionary*, 3 vols. (Westport, Connecticut: Greenwood Press, 1983). See for members of the jury: James Bowdoin, Mather Byles, Charles Chauncy, Samuel Cooper, Andrew Elliot, Joseph Green, Thomas Hutchinson, Samuel Mather, Ebenezer Mackintosh, and Edward Pemberton.

America, and he was a generous supporter of efforts to help the poor.

The Honorable John Erving: John Erving, eighty-two, the oldest juror, a native of Scotland, arrived in Boston around 1706, and rose to be a wealthy merchant. In 1720 he married Abigail Phillips, member of a prominent Welsh family. The Honorable Robert C. Winthrop said of him in 1845: "[A] few dollars earned on a commencement day, by ferrying passengers over the Charles River, shipped to Lisbon in the shape of fish, and from thence home to London in the shape of fruit, and thence home to Boston to be reinvested in fish, laid the foundation of the largest fortune of the day." He served as a member of the jury.

The Honorable James Pitts: Early sixties. He was an eminent merchant and a graduate of Harvard in 1731. He served as a member of the jury.

The Honorable Harrison Gray: Mid-forties. He was a member of the Boston Board of Selectman and a prominent abolitionist and staunch loyalist, and served as a member of the jury.

The Honorable James Bowdoin: Mid-forties. He is a member of the Massachusetts House of Representatives. He would later become a member of the Massachusetts Constitutional Convention. He was a member of the jury.

Joseph Green, Esq.: Late sixties – he is a well-known Boston wit and satirist, and was a friend of the then late Alexander

Pope. He was the owner of a brewery and also known as Josey Green. Would later be elected a member of the Committee of Correspondence on May 30, 1775. He served as a member of the jury.

Richard Carey: In 1772, 1773, and 1774, the town appointed a committee on the supply of the pulpit consisting of Richard Carey and others. These committees developed the liturgies. In 1772, the Tate and Brady version of the Psalms with Dr. Watt's Hymns was adopted for the use of the church. During the provincial phase, the scriptures were not read in the churches except in connection with exposition. He is a member of the jury.

The Rev. Charles Chauncy, D.D.: Sixty-seven. He is a member of the committee on the supply of the pulpit, prominent writer on theological matters, the pastor of the Old South Meeting House, and a member of the jury.

The Rev. Mather Byles, D.D. Sixty-six, he is a prominent writer and preacher of the time, friend of Alexander Pope. He was the punster of his age and his most famous pun said shortly after the Boston Massacre, "*which is better—to be ruled by one tyrant three thousand miles away, or by three thousand tyrants not a mile away?*" He is a member of the jury.

The Rev. Edward Pemberton, D.D.: Mid sixties, prominent member of the cloth and minister, he served, as a member of the jury.

The Rev. Andrew Elliot, D.D.: Early fifties. In 1742, was settled in the New North Church and served as pastor for thirty-six years. Graduated from Harvard in 1737. He was honored for his wisdom and manliness. He took a prominent and aggressive part in the Episcopal controversy, and was the friend of many learned men and a member of the jury.

The Rev. Samuel Cooper, D.D.: Late forties. Graduated from Harvard in 1743. Was called to succeed his father in May, 1746 as pastor of the Brattle Street Church in Boston. Copley painted him. He is a member of the jury.

The Rev. Samuel Mather, D.D.: Late sixties. He is the son of Cotton Mather, and pastor of the Tenth Congregational Church. He graduated from Harvard in 1723. In 1732, he was called to be a colleague of Mr. Gee at Second Church. A rift broke out. The junior pastor was accused of being not entirely sound in doctrine and not entirely proper in his conduct. He was eventually dismissed, and ninety-three of the church withdrew with him. Two hundred sixty-three remained. The separatists erected their own church, which became the Tenth Congregational Church in Boston. He continued to minister to his church until his death in 1785, when, in accordance with his request, most of his people returned to Second Church. The meetinghouse was later sold to the Universalists. He was a member of the jury.

The Rev. John Moorhead: Mid sixties. In 1727, a colony of Irish Presbyterians formed a church and began to worship in a plain wooden building, which had been used as a ("Gown"), in Long Lane, now Federal Street. He was their minister for a very long period, and he was a member of the jury. He died soon after the trial in 1773, and Phillis Wheatley wrote an elegy entitled "To Miss Mary Moorehead, On the Death of her Father, The Rev. Mr. John Moorehead."

Ebenezer Mackintosh: Thirty-six, a cobbler by profession. He served with the Boston Fire Department where he gained a reputation for rowdiness and quick temper. This reputation brought him to the attention of Boston's South End gang. Before long he was the leader of both the North End and South End gangs. Sam Adams recruited him for the Sons of Liberty where he quickly rose to leadership roles. He was slight of build and always dressed like a gentleman.

One thing that can be said of this group of men who gathered in the Common House in Boston is that, while they shared common interests—in that they were all from Boston, many of them ministers of the Gospel, a number of successful merchants, some aspiring poets and men of letters, and some related to one another—they were at the same time deeply divided on the key issues of the day: e.g., religious doctrine, the questions of politics, and slavery.

The colonial period of pre-Revolutionary Massachusetts is characterized by the religious differences of the time. The Puritans, while fleeing what they perceived as the corruption of the official Church of England, the Anglican Church, did not embrace the precept of freedom of religion once they were established in America. So small was their tolerance for independent religious thought that church member Ann

Hutchinson was banished from Massachusetts for committing the grievous heresy of believing in a Covenant of Grace instead of a Covenant of Works.

But religious heresy and controversy weren't confined to the Puritans of a century before; these issues were present in the room when these prominent men gathered that day in 1772. For example, Charles Chauncy was an articulate writer and speaker of the day, whose most well known sermons at that time were outspoken tracts against the religious controversies spawned by the "Great Awakening," or "New Light." Often writing pointedly against Jonathan Edwards, the intellectual leader of the awakening, Chauncey wrapped himself and other "Old Light" ministers in the mantle of reason and attacked the supporters of the revivals as men who foolishly believed that the Christian faith could be defined by the hysterical behavior initiated by George Whitefield, James Davenport, and others. In works such as *Enthusiasm Described and Cautioned Against, Seasonable Thoughts, and Ministers Cautioned,* he loudly warned against the theological and ecclesiastical results toward which the revivals tended.[6] At the same time, Phillis, and the Wheatleys were much moved by Whitefield and the "Great Awakening" movement. Furthermore, Phillis's sponsor in England, the Countess of Huntingdon, was perhaps Whitefield's most prominent supporter. Finally, it can be said that, while there was much to divide the various religious beliefs at the time, all these religious movements were united in their deep and abiding distrust, fear, and hatred of the Church of Rome.

---

6 Levemier and Wilmes, eds., *American Writers Before 1800*, 3 vols.

On the political front, Cooper, Bowdoin, Hancock, and others eventually were to become American patriots; Hutchinson, Oliver, Gray, Green, Byles, and John Wheatley, among others, all remained staunch loyalists. For instance, as late as 1775, Harrison Gray, although an abolitionist, published a twenty-page pamphlet, *A Few Remarks upon Some of the Votes of the Continental Congress*, in which he called colonial opposition to British control a "horrible rebellion" whose "ringleaders...may meet with the punishment that their crimes do justly deserve." Phillis disagreed with Gray, though they were in accord regarding the slavery issue.[7]

A word about casting: historical accuracy dictates the composition of the jury. The above descriptions of the jury members are more to show their place in their careers and in the Boston community, in the perspective of the time, than to highlight each as an individual character in the drama. The members of the jury would all be dressed pretty much the same; that is, conservatively, in dark suits and white shirts as were appropriate for businessmen and ministers of the Gospel at that time. Indeed, rather than be considered individually, for the purposes of the action in the play, the jury can be viewed as a group, and as many as fourteen characters can be cast or as few as two, Joseph Green and Mather Byles, the members of the jury who have speaking roles. The set can be designed so that only the first row of jurors is visible to the audience, and that can be as few as the two jurors noted. It should be noted that I have taken a few liberties with the actual date of the trial for dramatic effect.

Finally, wherever possible, I have used the actual words of the characters.

---

[7] See William H. Robinson, ed., *Phillis Wheatley and Her Writings* (New York: Garland, 1984).

The Trial of Phillis Wheatley

ACT ONE

Scene One:

10:00 p.m., Wednesday, November 4, 1772, Phillis's bedroom in the Wheatley mansion, Boston.

Scene Two:

11:00 p.m., the same evening, John Wheatley's study/fitting room.

ACT TWO

Scene One:

8:00 a.m., Thursday, November 5, 1772, the Governor's Council Chamber Room, the Common House, Boston.

Scene Two:

9:00 a.m., the same day, the Governor's Council Chamber Room.

Running time: two hours, including a fifteen-minute intermission.

Cast of Characters

Phillis Wheatley: Wheatley family household slave, eighteen.

Susanna Wheatley: Mistress of the Wheatley household, fifty-five.

John Wheatley: Master of the household, mid-sixties.

Mary Wheatley: Daughter of John and Susanna, twenty-nine.

Nathaniel Wheatley: her twin brother, twenty-nine.

Thomas Hutchinson: Last civilian governor, Province of Massachusetts Bay Colony, sixty-one.

Andrew Oliver: Last civilian lieutenant governor, Province of Massachusetts Bay Colony, sixty-six.

Thomas Hubbard: Deacon at the Old South Church, forty-five.

John Erving: Eminent Boston merchant, eighty-two.

James Pitts: Eminent Boston merchant, sixty.

Harrison Gray: Selectman of Boston, forty-six.

James Bowdoin: Member of the Governor's Council, forty-eight.

John Hancock, Esq.: Member of the Massachusetts House of Representatives and Governor's Council, thirty-five.

Ebenezer Mackintosh: Charismatic leader of waterfront thugs, shoemaker, thirty-six.

MEMBERS OF THE JURY:

Joseph (Josey) Green: Boston wit, sixty-seven

Richard Carey, D.D., mid-sixties.

Rev. Charles Chauncy, D.D., sixty-seven.

Rev. Mather Byles, D.D., sixty-six.

Rev. Edward Pemberton, D.D., mid-sixties.

Rev. Andrew Elliot, D.D., early fifties.

Rev. Samuel Cooper, D.D., late forties.

Rev. Samuel Mather, D.D., late-sixties.

Rev. James Moorhead D.D., mid-sixties.

A Captain of the British Grenadier Guards

Bailiff/Clerk of the Court

ACT ONE

Scene One

SCENE

An upstairs bedroom in the Wheatley mansion in Boston.

TIME

Late night, November 4, 1772, the eve of Guy Fawkes Day, celebrated as Pope's Day in Boston.

We are in a small but comfortable bedroom on the second story of the Wheatley mansion. It is Phillis's bedroom.

AT RISE

Phillis is seated in a chair at a desk. There is a single candle on the desk. Phillis is holding a quill pen poised over an inkwell and a sheaf of papers. She wears a simple gray frock, and a small white cap crowns her head. She sits unmoving, looking ahead. She is lost in concentration. There is a bed near the desk. Sitting on the bed is Mary Wheatley. She is holding an open book, and there are some more open books next to her on the bed.

PHILLIS

What am I to do?

MARY

You are exhausted.

PHILLIS

It is not the exhaustion of the body, but of the mind, that I fear.

MARY

You will do just fine. The best thing for you now is rest and sleep.

PHILLIS

Oh, Mary, I am not ready. I am not nearly prepared. How can I face those men tomorrow? I would rather be tied to that Hell Fire Red whipping post nigh,

(Pointing toward the window)

and receive thirty stripes than go before those eminent men tomorrow—to be tested.

(Pauses)

I am sorry, Mary,

(Regaining her composure)

my confidence fails me.

(Pauses)

Please, let's continue.

MARY

(Staring at the candle flame)

See how the candle burns down. You are like that candle.

(Pauses)

Soon the clock chimes will toll the eleventh hour. It is time to close the books, and extinguish the candle.

PHILLIS

(Musing)

"Bell, book, and candle." Dr. Faustus – Christopher Marlowe. It is the ancient rite of excommunication.

MARY

See, how you can pick things up. I wasn't ever thinking of Mr. Marlowe's play. You see, Phillis, your resources are a deep well that you can always draw from.

PHILLIS

Excommunication . . . It is a form of banishment.

MARY

Indeed. But now I am worried about you.

PHILLIS

Why, Mary?

MARY

Even now you are starting to cough again.

PHILLIS

Oh, Mary, when I contemplate my muses—Shakespeare, and Alexander

Pope; John Donne and John Milton!
Sometimes I have to catch my breath,
and it makes me cough.

MARY

Father said Mather Byles will be there
tomorrow, and he knew Alexander Pope.

PHILLIS

To think I will be in the presence of
someone who actually met Mr. Pope. I
shudder when I contemplate tomorrow.
I will appear before the royal governor
and lieutenant governor of the colony,
and
Mr. James Bowdoin and Mr. Hancock.

(Pauses)

Mary, sometimes, in a way, I feel
like I have been accused of some hei-
nous crime like Anne Hutchinson, the
Governor's great, great grandmother.

MARY

Nonsense — just the opposite.
Phillis, you know why you have been
summoned.

PHILLIS

Yes, to prove that I wrote my poems. To
be tested.

(Pausing)

It seems strange that it must be so —and yet it is—and before such eminent men of Boston. In the past these tests have been ordeals. And those who fail are banished.

MARY

Fair judges all — and God-fearing — many are men of the cloth whom you admire. You know their names: the Reverends Charles Chauncy, John Moorhead, Andrew Elliot, Samuel Cooper, and Samuel Mather.

PHILLIS

Cotton Mather's son — Biblical scholars all. How can I answer their questions?

MARY

Hancock, Hutchinson, and Oliver.

PHILLIS

(Repeating, chanting)

Hancock, Hutchinson, and Oliver.

MARY

Phillis, the Bible was the first book we put into your hands. You were reading and understanding even the most difficult passages within a year and a half of your coming to live with us. You can answer any questions on the sacred scriptures. I know you are prepared.

PHILLIS

I will feel so alone before these awesome eminences.

MARY

You will have supporters there. Mr. Wheatley, and Nathaniel. The Reverend Chauncy knows you. Some of the others will know of you from the elegies you wrote that were published in the *Gazette*. Mother will be there, and so will I.

PHILLIS

If only my memory were better. If they asked me to recite one of those elegies, I fear I would not be able to do it.

MARY

Phillis, have confidence. Just make it easy, like:

PHILLIS

(Chanting)

Hancock, Hutchinson, and Oliver.

MARY

That's it.

PHILLIS

(Becoming serious)

But you know that sometimes I forget.
Try with all my might, I cannot recall
years of my past before coming to live in
this home.

MARY

My dear Phillis, some parts of your
life that you have forgotten have been
blotted out for your own good. There are
remnants though. You told me how you
remember your mother pouring water
out of a jar as the sun rose.

PHILLIS

A phantom memory — a fleeting glimpse
as of a spirit.

MARY

Some things are too awful to remember.
When I think of your being snatched
from your parents, your captivity, the
Atlantic passage! We have no experience
with these terrible events. It does not
mean that you have a weak memory.

(Pausing)

We all have parts of our past we would like
to erase, but none so nightmarish as yours.
These events are best forgotten. You have
a fine memory for the task tomorrow. You
have been tested many times.

PHILLIS

When?

MARY

When Mother took you to her friends' homes and you recited your own poetry, as well as the sonnets of Shakespeare, passages from Alexander Pope, and other immortal poets. Now, enough of this self-doubt.

(Pausing)

I know what...

PHILLIS

What?

MARY

Let's pretend you are there right now – in the room before the assembled men.

PHILLIS

Yes!

MARY

Now, imagine that I am the Reverend Elliot.

PHILLIS

Oh, this is fun.

MARY

Are you ready?

PHILLIS

Yes, Reverend Elliot.

MARY

Now, Phillis,
(Changing her voice to make it sound deeper)
what is your favorite passage from the Old Testament?
(Mimicking)
Oh — you don't —

Rising from her chair, Phillis slowly begins to recite.

PHILLIS

"By the rivers of Babylon, there we sat down, yea, we wept, when we remembered Zion. We hanged our harps upon the willows in the midst thereof.
For there they that carried us away captive required of us a song; and they that wasted us required of us mirth, saying, Sing us one of the songs of Zion.
How shall we sing the Lord's song in a strange land?"

Mary gestures for Phillis to sit.

MARY

(Still feigning, suppressing a smile)

Very good, Ms. Phillis, it is a psalm?

PHILLIS

(Sitting down)

Sir, I like to think of it as a song. I sing the ancient song of those in exile. Sir, the Old Testament is a story of the people of Israel and how when they strayed from God's teachings they found themselves in exile.

MARY

And are you in exile here?

PHILLIS

Sir, I was snatched from my native soil. But here I feel I am part of a family. I pray that I have not strayed from God's law, that I have not broken the covenant as did the ancient Israelites.

MARY

(Using her normal voice)

Phillis, be careful to answer only what is posed.

PHILLIS

It just came to me—I'm sorry.

MARY

I know you witnessed the riot that killed the Snider boy, and but a month later the massacre, and those events have left their mark. Be careful not to digress tomorrow into recent events in Boston.

PHILLIS

But, Mary, I have memorialized these events in my poetry. My elegies on the death of Christopher Snider and on the massacre.

MARY

They are in your manuscript for all to see, yes. Just be careful to avoid the politics of the day.

(Changing her voice to that of the inquisitor)

Now, Miss Phillis, give me an example of a story of exile in the Old Testament.

PHILLIS

The book of Daniel, sir.

MARY

What of the book of Daniel do you know?

PHILLIS

Oh, sir, the book of Daniel is poetry to me. The people of Israel had been taken from the Promised Land and were in exile in Babylon. King Nebuchadnezzar summoned the best of the young captives—Shadrach, Meshach, and Abednego—to be brought before him. Seated on his throne, he asked them:

(Pointing)

Is it true that you do not serve my gods or worship the image of gold that I have set up?

MARY

"Youths of noble birth without blemish, handsome and skillful in all wisdom."

PHILLIS

And how they put their faith in the God of Israel and chose to walk into the fiery furnace where — to the amazement of the king — the angel of God led them through the flames unscathed.

MARY

(Dropping the feigned voice of the interrogator)

And so it will be with you.

PHILLIS

When I walk into the fiery furnace tomorrow.

MARY

You will be like...

PHILLIS

(Picking up the beat)

Shadrach, Meshach, and Abednego.

MARY

(Joining in the rhythm)

Just like Shadrach, Meshach, and Abednego.

PHILLIS

Like Chauncy, Cooper, Moorhead, and Mather.

MARY

Cotton Mather's son.

PHILLIS

But I should also be like Daniel.

MARY

Standing before:

PHILLIS

Hancock, Hutchinson, and Oliver.

MARY

And Daniel could read the handwriting on the wall.

(Pausing)

That reminds me, they might ask you to write something on a subject of their choice while they watch. They might even ask you to compose a poem.

PHILLIS

That would be a blessing. It would take time from other probing.

(Coughing into her handkerchief)

Oh, Mary, what if they ask me to explain my muse?

MARY

Are you sure you are all right?

PHILLIS

(Coughing subsiding)

Yes, it is the excitement of the moment.

MARY

I know when you get tired. You haven't changed. It's just like when you were a little girl. It's time for sleep.

PHILLIS

(Sitting down in her chair)

Oh, Mary, the bell has not tolled. If only they could come here and let me recite for them in our home, like your friends. I would be confident. It's just to think that I have to go to the Common House and stand before all those men.

Mary looks to the window rattled by a blast of frozen rain.

MARY

I wish I could spare you even going outside in this storm. The storm grows more fierce. Father said it is a nor'easter.

Phillis looks around the room.

PHILLIS

This is the only home that I know. Here, I feel so comfortable, so secure, I can write. My muses come to me here.

(Rising)

But when I venture out the door, the people on the streets — they don't know me as you do. I know they see me in a different light. Other slaves — they too, see me as a stranger. I know what they are thinking. I appear different. I am not one of them.

MARY

Phillis, my dear, that is why we —you — must publish these poems. So you will have an audience beyond these walls. When you walk out the front door, everyone will see you and they will say: "There goes Phillis Wheatley. Did you know that she is a poet and has published a book of poetry?"

PHILLIS

Mary, fame — no — that is not my desire. I love to write. I need to write. But I do it for myself and for this family, and some others. I am happy just writing poems in this home for you and the family.

MARY

But, Phillis, it is not entirely your choice to make. So many in Boston have already read or heard your poetry that has been published in the *Gazette.* You have an audience. The elegies that you write when beloved family members pass — those elegies bring great comfort to the families. The recipients have all been grateful and amazed that one so young could have such insights on their grief.

PHILLIS

Sometimes it is only when I write of death that I feel truly free.

MARY

Phillis! Whatever do you mean?

PHILLIS

It is as inexplicable as a muse. It is in this room that the natural and the supernatural coexist.

MARY

(Puzzled)

I think I understand.

PHILLIS

Yet, at the same time, I fear the world as much for the pleasure it offers. I fear that I may want to become famous. I know that is the sin of pride. And, as we know, pride goeth before a fall.

MARY

(Pausing)

There is more beyond both fear and pride, and that is our duty to ourselves and to God to fulfill our destiny. When you confront these demons of fear and pride — remember that God calls some of us to be pioneers. Just like he called Moses to lead the ancient Israelites out of the bondage of Pharaoh. God is calling you. And when God calls us and we obey, we can be assured that he will stand with us, though we walk into a fiery furnace.

(Smiling)

Like...

PHILLIS

Shadrach, Meshach, and Abednego.

MARY

Or walk into a lion's den, like...

PHILLIS

Daniel.

MARY

Or stand before...

PHILLIS

Chauncy, Cooper, Moorhead, and Mather.

Mary and Phillis laugh.

MARY

And be more clever than...

PHILLIS

The magicians, the enchanters, the sorcerers, and the Chaldeans.

MARY

(Moved)

"On the fifth day of the fourth month..."

PHILLIS

(Picking up the quote)

"Of King Jehoiachin's exile, the word of the Lord came to the priest Ezekiel, the son of Buzi, in the land of the Chaldeans by the river Chebar — there the hand of the Lord came upon me."

MARY

And so it has come upon you. You are ready for tomorrow. I know it now.

PHILLIS

Please, Mary, you are always a source of inspiration to me. I know what I must do. Help me to prepare a little more. Please, Mary. And the clock bell has not yet tolled the hour.

MARY

(In the moment)

Oh, just a little more, but then to bed. We don't want to wake up Mother. She needs her rest.

Phillis returns to her chair at the desk.

PHILLIS

Sometimes I feel that I am to blame for that.

MARY

For what?

PHILLIS

For the mistress's failing health. I have been a burden to her all these years when she could have had someone helping her. Instead, she had me to take care of. If it weren't for me, your mother would still have her health.

MARY

Phillis, you mustn't say that. You have never been a heavy burden. And to see what you have become is one of Mother's greatest joys and accomplishments. Now, let's practice a little longer.

PHILLIS

Oh, thank you, Mary.

MARY

Now, I want you to give me something different this time. Remember, I may have already given you a question on this author.

PHILLIS

I understand.

MARY

John Donne.

PHILLIS

"Go and catch a falling star, get with child a mandrake root, tell me, where all past years are, or who cleft the Devil's foot.
Teach me to hear mermaids singing, and find what wind serves to advance an honest mind."

MARY

When you recite that, I hear music.

PHILLIS

It is the music of the spirit.

MARY

Or is it music of the spheres?

PHILLIS

The spheres?

MARY

The mysteries of the universe, of God's majesty, of eternity, of the Divine.

(Feigning the interrogator)

Now, Phillis, what is the meaning of this poem that you have just recited?

PHILLIS

It's a song, sir. Not everything has to mean something.

MARY

But something can mean everything. There is meaning there, Phillis, what is it?

PHILLIS

The meaning, sir, is revealed later.

MARY

(Feigning)

Pray, Phillis, reveal to us — the jury — the hidden meaning now.

PHILLIS

"If thou be'ist born to strange sights, things invisible to see, ride ten thousand days and nights, till age snow white hairs on thee; thou, when thou return'st, wilt tell me all strange wonders that befell thee, and swear no where lives a woman true and fair."

MARY

(As inquisitor)

Does that mean that Mr. Donne did not hold women in a very high regard?

PHILLIS

Indeed, sir, it means that Mr. Donne was disappointed in love.

MARY

(Pleased, and in her normal voice)

At least you did not address the Reverend Elliot as "Old Mole," as Hamlet did to Horatio.

PHILLIS

(With a broad grin)

I did not say Old Mole, as Hamlet called Horatio.

(Pausing, serious)

But what if they press me, Mary? About the meaning of Mr. Donne's poem.

MARY

Then tell them...

PHILLIS

What?

MARY

Well, just tell them that it is what you are trying to do — to catch a falling star.

PHILLIS

Oh, Mary.

MARY

This, little sister, is the last one. See how the candle burns low and the light dims.

PHILLIS

Please, Mary, don't say that.

MARY

Why not?

PHILLIS

I don't know. It's just that, when you said those words, it was like a shadow passing before me, like a premonition. It made me think that someone in this house might die.

MARY

We will all pass to glory someday, Phillis. This storm will pass. For all we know, by tomorrow afternoon when we emerge from the Common House, the sun may be shining.

Mary picks up a book from the bed.

MARY

Now, and this is the very last thing. I will read a passage and you tell me the author.

PHILLIS

I am ready.

MARY

Here is one:
"When once our heav'nly-guided soul shall climb, then all this earthly gross-ness quit, attired with stars, we shall forever sit, triumphing over death, and chance and thee old time."

PHILLIS

Too easy. John Milton. But my favorite is...

A gentle knocking. Enter Susanna Wheatley, dressed in a nightgown, with an afghan over her shoulders. She appears pale, and is carrying a glass of water.

SUSANNA

Mary! Phillis should be in bed! She has studied enough for this cold night.

(To Phillis)

Now you need your rest for tomorrow. I heard you coughing. Take this water.

Phillis takes the glass.

PHILLIS

I am sorry if I woke you, Mistress. I know you need your sleep.

SUSANNA

Phillis, dear, I will have plenty of time to sleep. I have been so worried about your health.

PHILLIS

You should not worry.

SUSANNA

Not worry? You are still sick. Why, just a few months ago I was afraid ...

Phillis drops to her knees.

PHILLIS

It has pleased God to lay me on a bed of sickness — and a few months ago, I knew naught but my deathbed — but he has been graciously pleased to restore me in a good measure.

SUSANNA

God will do his part and you must do your part. Now you must sleep. It's drafty in here. The wind is so fierce that it penetrates the windowpanes; I feel it. Let me put this over your shoulders.

Susanna removes the afghan and places it over Phillis's shoulders.

PHILLIS

Oh, Mistress, it is you who need that more than I. And it is I who should be serving you.

Phillis tries to hand it back, protesting.

SUSANNA

Now, now, you needn't worry about me.

Susanna places it carefully over Phillis's shoulders.

PHILLIS

Oh, Mistress, I pray that I may be made thankful for God's corrections, and that I may make proper use of them — especially tomorrow — to the glory of his grace.

SUSANNA

Yes, yes. But now you need sleep more than anything.

PHILLIS

"Sleep that knits up the raveled sleeve of care."

MARY

"Thy best of rest is sleep."

PHILLIS

"And that thou oft provok'st, yet grossly fear'st thy death which is no more."

Phillis still kneels, with her head bowed, as if in prayer.

MARY

Well said.

SUSANNA

Phillis, I only wish that I could spare you the ordeal you must endure.

PHILLIS

(Rising)

God willing — I will do more than endure.

SUSANNA

Yes, you will. Did I hear you two laughing?

PHILLIS

Or was it mermaids singing?

SUSANNA

What?

MARY

(Inquisitor voice)

What does it mean, "mermaids singing"?

PHILLIS

Oh, just a line from a song, sir.

Phillis and Mary laugh at their private joke; Phillis begins to cough into her handkerchief.

SUSANNA

(Distressed)

You are coughing again. Did you cough up any blood? Let me see your handkerchief.

PHILLIS

Just a trace. It is embarrassing to me.

SUSANNA

Doctor Stone wants me to tell him if you cough up any blood.

PHILLIS

It was nothing.

SUSANNA

Look at you! You are so weakened from this. I can't ask you to go before those men coughing like this. You can't go out into this storm.

PHILLIS

Oh, Mistress, I must go. I may feel weak, but I have faith that if my flesh and my heart fail me, God will be my strength.

MARY

Mother, we were practicing. Phillis, tell Mother what you are going to do tomorrow.

PHILLIS

What?

MARY

What you are going to catch?

PHILLIS

(Brightening)

Catch? Oh, yes, madam, a star — a fall-ing star. I'm going to catch a falling star.

MARY

And what are you going to hear?

PHILLIS

Why, I am going to hear mermaids singing.

SUSANNA

You two have been up to your word games again, I see.

MARY

Mother, we were practicing one last time. Phillis was just going to bed. I was playing the role of the Reverend Elliot.

PHILLIS

And I was playing me, as if I were there before them all.

SUSANNA

Well, now I am playing your mistress, and you need to sleep.

PHILLIS

Truly, Mistress.

MARY
And Phillis is as prepared now as she ever will be for their questions.

SUSANNA
Do you feel strong enough, Phillis?

PHILLIS
I do.

MARY
And just imagine! Tomorrow, when Phillis is able to convince these eminent men that she is indeed the author of her manuscript, then the barriers to publishing it will tumble like the walls of Jericho.

PHILLIS
And the truth will be like a trumpet. Like Joshua's trumpet.

MARY
And Phillis will be the first Negro woman to publish a book of poetry in America.

SUSANNA
Maybe in the world!

MARY
I have a feeling about tomorrow.

SUSANNA

A feeling?

MARY

I don't know — something. How can I explain? But I feel that tomorrow will be important in ways that none of us can fully comprehend right now.

SUSANNA

Now, we see through a glass darkly.

MARY

I know, mother, but my feeling is that perhaps with all our blessings, with our place in society, this family will not be remembered for those things.

SUSANNA

There is a reason for that — if we are successful.

MARY

You share my feeling?

SUSANNA

Because books live on after we have all gone to glory. Like the ancient Roman inscription reads: "In mortal books there dwell immortal minds."

MARY

Yes — yes, that is part of my feeling. Phillis published! Just imagine, Phillis, you may be the only one of us who is remembered.

PHILLIS

If I am remembered, it will not be to my glory, but to yours.

SUSANNA

It will be to your glory and to the glory of God.

MARY

Amen. And they who do not believe will be the less for it.

SUSANNA

The publishers did not believe because they felt that others would not believe — and there would be no buyers for the book.

MARY

Why does everything have to be so difficult? Why can't they just accept that Phillis is capable of writing this material? It is laid before them, yet they do not believe.

PHILLIS

It will only take one to doubt, and not sign.

MARY

And if such a doubter is present, and even if you spoke with the tongue of angels and had the gift of prophesy, you would still be as sounding brass to him.

SUSANNA

That is why you — we — must have faith.

(Pausing)

Some may see me as a promoter who will do anything to advance Phillis.

MARY

For what reason?

SUSANNA

To advance a cause.

MARY

What cause?

SUSANNA

The cause of those who call for the abolition of slavery, for example.

MARY

(Surprised)

We cannot deny that perhaps half the men who will gather in that room tomorrow support that cause.

PHILLIS

I fear that I am the cause of this. A family whose word has never been doubted before, and now, because of me, this family must be tested publicly. My master and mistress must also be tested as never before, and you, Mary, and Nathaniel.

SUSANNA

Phillis, it is not you that has caused us any distress. We are so proud of you.

MARY

Phillis, you must never blame yourself. There is bound to be some resentment by ignorant people that your accomplishments do not match your station in life, but such people will not be present tomorrow.

(Becoming animated)

This is the time of testing, not just for Phillis, or for us, but for Boston — indeed, for America. You only have to go out on the streets, read the signs; everyone's beliefs are being tested!

SUSANNA

My dear little Phillis, I want you to remember always that you have as fine an education as there is in Boston for a woman your age.

PHILLIS

I have you, Mary, this family to thank for that.

SUSANNA

We all helped, but God blessed you with a brilliant mind. And somehow he brought you to us. You have worked hard and taken advantage of this opportunity that He has presented you. And remember, Phillis, no one can take your education away from you.

MARY

You are the proof that women can write poetry as well as men.

SUSANNA

And you are living proof that Africans can make as fine a contribution to the arts as anyone.

MARY

That is really what is being tested.

SUSANNA

(Brightening)

Here we've been so disappointed that Phillis was rejected by the publishers in Boston. But, we should never forget that she has a powerful champion in England —Selina Hastings, Countess of Huntingdon. Phillis, you made such an impression on her when you sent her the elegy that you wrote on the death of the Reverend Whitehead.

PHILLIS

It is hard to believe that it was almost two years ago to this day that he died. I can still see him standing in the pulpit at the Old South Church and hear the words.

SUSANNA

The countess has agreed to have your book dedicated to her when it is published — and it will be published.

PHILLIS

It was thanks to her ladyship that the Reverend Whitehead was able to come to America and share with us his vision of the "New Light." I am forever grateful that I was honored to hear him preach — and to think that he died on that tour of America.

MARY

It was his sacrifice for us. And we must remember his message that we have to have faith. True faith will prevail over the new philosophies that put reason over it. Phillis, do you remember what you wrote in your elegy upon his death? Surely they will ask.

PHILLIS

"He longed to see America excel; he charged its youth that every grace divine arise, and in their actions shine."

SUSANNA

Phillis, isn't that what we are doing now? You are letting your light shine forth. Tomorrow you will be a bright light before those men. You will be an example of how the youth of America can excel.

Mary seats herself on the other side of Phillis on the bed.

PHILLIS

And if I fail tomorrow, the manuscript will be stillborn. I will die without having brought to life that which I love.

MARY

Phillis, you are prepared.
Mother, have you told Phillis?

SUSANNA

About?

Mary makes a wavelike motion with her hands.

SUSANNA

Oh, that. It was going to be a surprise.

PHILLIS

(Curious)

What?

MARY

(To her mother)

What we talked about.

PHILLIS

Is it about Nathaniel? Did something happen?

MARY

No, not about Nathaniel. He will be there tomorrow.

PHILLIS

I worry about him, with all the unrest on the streets, and he is so often out there.

MARY

Please, mother, now is the time to tell her. If not now, when, what better time?

SUSANNA

Of course, Mary, you are right.

PHILLIS

Oh, Mistress, please tell me.

SUSANNA

Phillis, you have been dreaming of meeting her ladyship?

PHILLIS

Oh yes, so much so.

SUSANNA

Well, in a few months, and God willing, it will come to pass, no matter the outcome of the trial tomorrow.

(Pausing)

Doctor Stone said an ocean voyage in the spring with the fresh sea air would be the best thing for your health.

PHILLIS

(Smiling)

Oh my!

SUSANNA

Mr. Wheatley and I are planning to have Nathaniel accompany you to England, on the *London Packet*, in April. We have sent a letter to her ladyship, who will, no doubt, contact other prominent people in England who have heard of your work.

MARY

You may even meet the King and Queen.

PHILLIS

(Glowing)

I cannot imagine.

MARY

It is true. Now, we just have to get through tomorrow.

PHILLIS

(Animated)

Oh, how I wish this would pass.

SUSANNA

Soon it will be the happiest and most blessed season of the birth of our Savior. By then this will be behind us. And we will all be happy at home — together.

MARY

And we can look forward to the publication of Phillis's manuscript and her trip to England.

PHILLIS

If it is God's will.

SUSANNA

Think of yourself as David as he went forth in a righteous cause against Goliath.

MARY

Do you remember your poem about David and Goliath?

PHILLIS

"Goliath of Gath."

SUSANNA

When you walk into that room tomorrow, picture David as he walked out on that plain so long ago and stood before the giant —Goliath. Have faith that, just as God empowered David to step forward to the ordeal and prevail against the giant, He will give you the power to make the truth prevail.

PHILLIS

Oh, Mistress, I fear that my mind may go blank. What if I can't even remember my name?

SUSANNA

Nonsense.

MARY

Please try, Phillis.

SUSANNA

My favorite lines from that poem,

(Pausing)

the words that you put into David's mouth when Goliath was taunting him on the plain, with the armies of both sides looking on: "Thy spear and shield..."

Phillis drops to her knees and joins in the recitation.

PHILLIS

"Shall no protection to thy body yield: Jehovah's name — no other arms I bear, I ask no other in this glorious war. Today the Lord of Hosts will give Victory..."

Coughing, she stops the recitation.

SUSANNA

That is the spirit that will prevail!

PHILLIS

(Rising)
The spirit of David!

MARY

And the spirit of Daniel. And the spirit of...

PHILLIS AND MARY

(Chanting)
Shadrach, Meshach, and Abednego.
Chauncy, Cooper, Moorhead, and Mather.

SUSANNA

Now, to bed.

Susanna and Mary exit.

PHILLIS

"Bell, book and candle, candle book and bell,
forward and backward, to curse Faustus to hell." It is the ancient right of excommunications – banishment and exile.

BLACKOUT

ACT ONE

Scene Two

SCENE

John Wheatley's study/tailor studio in the Wheatley mansion. He is standing, adjusting a bright red military tunic with shiny brass buttons on a tailor's mannequin.

TIME

Later the same night.

Footfalls in the foyer.

JOHN

Nathaniel?

Nathaniel enters.

NATHANIEL

Father. Sorry I am late. I promise you that you have my undivided attention for the next twenty-four hours to help with Phillis - through her trial.

JOHN

Have you been hearing anything of tomorrow's trial?

NATHANIEL

No, it's as if no one knows of it. Lord Mansfield's ruling of four months ago is still the talk of the town. Incidentally, I obtained a copy of the actual ruling. The uplifting language might help us in preparing for Phillis's trial.

Nathaniel takes a folio from a pocket of his greatcoat. He holds it close to the light.

NATHANIEL

I circled the salient part - here it is: "The state of slavery is of such a nature, that it is incapable of being introduced on any reasons, moral or political, but only by positive law, which preserves its force long after the reasons, occasion, and time itself from whence it was created, is erased from memory. It is so odious, that nothing can be suffered to support it, but positive law. Whatever inconveniences, therefore, may follow from the decision, and though the Heavens may fall, I cannot say this case is allowed or approved by the law of England; and therefore the black must be discharged."

JOHN

"Though the Heavens may fall."

NATHANIEL

In the taverns and on the streets there is both fear and hope: fear of change, and hope in the hearts of the abolitionists. They ask if slavery is outlawed in England, then should this ruling not apply to the colonies — to us here in Boston? "Whatever inconveniences, therefore, may follow from the decision."

JOHN

Indeed, there is a Boston connection with the case. It was from this town that Mr. Stewart fled his custom's post for London taking his servant Somerset with him.

NATHANIEL

But, Father, the southern colonies would never accept a ruling from a court in England or from any other colony that frees the slaves. And even if Parliament were to codify the Mansfield ruling of June 22, in this current political atmosphere, it would be perceived as another edict on America, another regulation from the mother country limiting our independence of action as odious as the Stamp Act.

JOHN

It is a moot point. Parliament will never pass such a law. There are too many powerful interests to oppose it. The planters have lobbies before Parliament.

NATHANIEL

Would that this colony and our sister colonies had such powerful supporters in Parliament. We have no representation, but only taxation. We might as well be slaves to England here? We need Lord Mansfield to free us! Please, Lord Mansfield, free us. Let us go!

JOHN

(Shaking his head)

A dreadful night — and not just because of the storm. We are at the mercy of the forces of darkness. And I do not mean Parliament. Mackintosh and his so-called "Sons of Liberty" rule the streets.

(Frustrated)

The world is upside down.

NATHANIEL

(Musing)

"Listen to me and you shall hear, news hath not been this thousand year:

Since Herod, Caesar, and many more,
you never heard the like before.
Holy days are despis'd, new fashions are devis'd.
Old Christmas is kicked out of Town.
Yet let's be content, and the times lament, you see the world turn'd upside down."

JOHN

This is nothing to make light of, Nathaniel.

NATHANIEL

Is it not true?

John turns and points to the table next to the mannequin.

JOHN

Someone left a scroll at the doorstep and it is addressed to you. I don't know who left it. Perhaps, by one of these rabble who roam the streets. We are back to the mob rule of the sixties. But, let us lay these things aside for the moment. We have to finish Phillis's attestation tonight.

NATHANIEL

(Correcting with a smile)

You mean declaration, Father.

JOHN

Attestation — declaration — what is the difference?

NATHANIEL

Attestation smacks of dusty law books and dreary courtrooms.

(Exulting with a flourish)

Declaration is the stuff upon which nations are built.

JOHN

You and your French philosophers — your Rousseau, Voltaire, and . . .

NATHANIEL

Montesquieu!

JOHN

Sometimes I wonder if I did the right thing in sending you to Harvard.

NATHANIEL

(Smiling)

I will put the French philosophers out of my mind. I grant you —attestation.

Nathanial makes a courtly flourish.

JOHN

(With frustration)

We are not forming a nation this bitter night. We are trying to compose a paragraph in such a way that the men gathered tomorrow will put their names to it.

NATHANIEL

The result tomorrow will tell the world something of the kind of nation that we favor to be formed.

JOHN

(Frustrated)

All this talk of forming nations — is not King George our monarch? Are we not his loyal subjects? Is not the Province of Massachusetts Bay Colony our country?

NATHANIEL

A nation's first responsibility is to its people. I don't have to tell you that since the sixties, the Parliament has imposed upon this land ever-increasing tax burdens on our industry. The Grenville Act, the Writs of Assistance, the Stamp Act, and the Townsend Acts. These have sorely burdened the people and would destroy our commerce. They have not only failed but led to violence and to the bloody massacre itself just two years ago.

JOHN

And had you not taken Phillis out to see what all the ruckus was!

NATHANIEL

How could I not? The massacre occurred practically on our doorstep. Yes, it was shocking, and she saw it all. Our impressionable little Phillis was so moved she wrote of it.

JOHN

(Brightening)

Of course it is part of her manuscript for all to see. But we should be looking forward, not backward. Things are getting better now. Commerce is improving slowly. The boycott of English goods is over. The ships are sailing.

NATHANIEL

For now, but when we learn of the latest outrage.

JOHN

There will be none. So why start riling up what is best put behind us? This is now an opportunity for reconciliation with the mother county.

NATHANIEL

(Fatalistically)

I feel it is too late, father. What is done cannot be undone. When former Governor Bernard appointed Hutchinson governor, and chief justice of the Supreme Court, he not only bypassed James Otis Senior, and his son, who were both eminently qualified attorneys, but he changed this colony from a rule of law by courts, to a rule of the Governor by edict and with no appeal. Otis still bears a grudge against Hutchinson for that insult, and Sam Adams sides with Otis against both Hutchinson and his lieutenant governor, Oliver.

JOHN

Should personal grudges rule our land, our policies?

NATHANIEL

(With emotion)

How can we ignore tyranny? Hutchinson heads two branches of this government. I must stand with Otis and Adams on this matter. Each day I fear more edicts flaunting our charter, more bypassing of our legislature in making Executive appointments, more tyranny.

JOHN

Otis and that damnable Sam Adams *are* the rabble leaders! What is the difference between them and the likes of Mackintosh?

NATHANIEL

(Frustrated)

I shall speak no more on these matters.

There is a pause.

JOHN

(Changing the subject)

I've made some edits and I want to know your opinion. I want you to read it to me; I want to hear it read aloud.

NATHANIEL

We've already gone over your draft letter to the publishers.

John gestures to the envelope on the table next to the scroll.

JOHN

That is my statement of Phillis's history since your mother took her from the ship eleven years ago, and of her remarkable progress under our tutelage in this home. I am prepared to be questioned on it. If you would just read the part that they will put their names to.

Picking up the document from the table, Nathaniel clears his throat and holds the broadsheet up to the light.

NATHANIEL

"We whose names are underwritten, do assure the world, that the poems specified in the following page, were (as we verily believe) written by Phillis, a young Negro girl, who was but a few years since, brought an uncultivated barbarian from Africa and has ever since been, and now is, under the disadvantage of serving as a slave in a family in this town. She has been examined by some of the best judges and is thought qualified to write them."

JOHN

That sounds good. What do you think?

Nathaniel sits down at the table with the broadsheet before him, and reads.

NATHANIEL

Good. Good.

JOHN

I wanted to ask you before making changes. Do you suppose the unequivocal language may put them off?

NATHANIEL

There can be no equivocation, no consensus statement, no footnote, no abstentions. It must be unanimous. It must be unequivocal. Those who come to test must also attest. Attestations, declarations, are by their very nature final and damn—

JOHN

(Interrupting)

Nathaniel—your language.

NATHANIEL

Sorry, Father, I was caught up with emotion suddenly. But I ask you —did Lord Mansfield equivocate when he said that even the air of England is too pure to tolerate slavery? Principles have been compromised too long in England and too long in this Province.

John shakes his head fatalistically.

JOHN

The air of England?

NATHANIEL

(Making an edit at the desk)

I'm still worried about Mackintosh.

JOHN

What does that have to do with this?

NATHANIEL

The British troops will not intervene if there is a disruption tomorrow. With the Pope's Day celebration, I fear they will avoid confrontation — they do not want another "massacre." They will have a token presence, but most will stay in their barracks across the street from the Common House.

JOHN

They would want to avoid another massacre, no doubt.

NATHANIEL

Remember, the massacre began with a confrontation between one British soldier and a boy, and rapidly spun out of control. We will be at the mercy of Mackintosh. Boston has long needed an organized constabulary.

JOHN

(Shaking his head)

This is not an auspicious beginning to Phillis's trial.

NATHANIEL
Perhaps you should try to postpone it?

JOHN
Nathaniel, you know what I had to go through to persuade these men to assemble at the Common House tomorrow.

NATHANIEL
Yes, but with this new threat—rumors of Mackintosh being outraged by the Mansfield decision.

JOHN
It's too late to change it now. These great lights will either come or not.

NATHANIEL
John Hancock is not one to back away from threats. If no one else comes, he will—in spite of Mackintosh.

John holds a needle up to the candle and tries to thread it with his other hand.

(Frustrated that he cannot thread the needle)

JOHN Let's not be bickering over Mackintosh. Come try on your coat. It is almost finished.

Nathaniel rises from the table and crosses to try on the jacket.

NATHANIEL

It's magnificent. I look like Captain Prescott.

JOHN

You are my son. You must make the family proud. Now, I want to check the fit. Please stand by the mirror.

NATHANIEL

Nathaniel moves to the mirror.

NATHANIEL

Attestation — declaration - attestation.

JOHN

What?

NATHANIEL

I was just thinking what fun Mary and Phillis would have with those words.

(Chanting lighheartedly)

At/tes/ta/tion—dec/la/ra/tion.

JOHN

Please stand still.

Nathaniel looks in the mirror, suddenly serious.

NATHANIEL

But, Father, this is an officer's coat. In the militia, the men elect their officers. I am only just beginning.

JOHN

Nonsense, they will elect you an officer. You are a Harvard man.

JOHN

(Frustrated)

Now take off the jacket. I want to make some adjustments. And please thread the needle for me.

Nathaniel takes the needle and thread.

NATHANIEL

Each day the British tighten their rule over us through their appointed lackeys like Hutchinson, and his handpicked lieutenant governor, Oliver. Hutchinson has become judge, jury, and chief executioner in this colony.

(Shaking his head)

And tomorrow he will sit in judgment of Phillis.

John places the uniform back on the mannequin.

JOHN

He is the royal governor and he will preside—that is all I care about.

(Rhetorically)

How could we have a gathering of the most eminent men in Boston and exclude the royal governor and his lieutenant?

NATHANIEL

You could not, of course. But Thomas Hutchinson has never even studied law. In choosing him as chief justice, Governor Bernard rejected John Adams and the entire Boston Bar to appoint a non-lawyer.

JOHN

Maybe that was a good idea. Look at John Adams — reviled now for defending the King's guard that fired on the mob on King's Street. Look at James Otis, a raving lunatic.

John crosses to the front of the uniform.

NATHANIEL

James Otis was passed over long before Hutchinson's appointment. But his words, "a man's house is his castle," still ring true. Only later was he beaten senseless in the British Coffee House and left a pathetic shadow of his former self.

JOHN

Otis should have avoided that notorious Tory Coffee House.

NATHANIEL

Of course — but what possessed him to go in there? He was objecting that we are ruled by the Parliament through its handpicked governor not capable of governing, a chief justice not schooled in the law, a man totally incapable by aptitude or interest of mastering the fundamentals of constitutional government — yet gathering all power to himself and bypassing this colony's legislature.

JOHN

We live under the Constitution of England and our charter. I thought we taught you better. You should be proud of your English heritage. In your philosophy is it not writ that we are either a nation of laws or we live in chaos?

NATHANIEL

If men like Thomas Hutchinson are the interpreters of the Constitution, then I see no difference between living under law or tyranny.

John stitches at the jacket on the mannequin, shaking his head in frustration.

JOHN

Bear in mind, Nathaniel, it wasn't just hard work that got me to my position — there's something else. I have been successful in business because people trust me. Do you know why that is?

NATHANIEL

It is because you are an honest and honorable man, and trust begets trust.

JOHN

It is because of one thing and one thing alone. My name. I have worked hard at my business, but I have also worked hard at keeping my name from notoriety and scandal. I have done that by being honest with people and being been very careful about what I put my name to.

Crossing to the table, John picks up the broadsheet.

NATHANIEL

I understand.

JOHN

Do you?

NATHANIEL

Yes. Perhaps, Father, you have taught me too well. I would ask you — why are we going to the Common House in the morning? Why have you gone to all this trouble to invite the most eminent men in Boston to attend this meeting?

JOHN

For Phillis, of course.

NATHANIEL

And what are you going to ask of them?

JOHN

What do you mean?

NATHANIEL

You are going to ask them that they give you — give Phillis — that most precious thing of which you speak: their names. You are asking them to sign their name to an attestation that it is their most sincere belief that Phillis is the author of her manuscript of poems, "On Subjects Religious and Moral."

Nathaniel crosses to his father at the table.

JOHN

Well?

He sets the broadsheet down on the desk.

NATHANIEL

Don't you see, Father? People will not believe in Phillis's cause unless she has credibility. By signing the declaration—

JOHN

(Raising his hand)

Attestation.

NATHANIEL

(Correcting himself)

Attestation. By signing this attestation, these most distinguished men of Boston are giving Phillis's cause credibility. No great cause has become successful without people putting their names to it.

NATHANIEL

(Shaking his head)

Lord Mansfield's decision is now part of the common law of England upon which our law is based. It is the beginning of the end of the old order.

JOHN

What effect will it have on Phillis, I wonder?

NATHANIEL

Phillis does not need a legal decision to inform her philosophy. And she is no doubt fully aware of the decision.

JOHN

Have you spoken with her about it?

NATHANIEL

No, not on the decision but I can read her inner struggle in her poetry.

JOHN

You must be reading things that I do not.

NATHANIEL

She has written so many of these elegies for our friends in Boston who have lost loved ones.

JOHN

And they are greatly admired.

NATHANIEL

Of course, and they bring consolation to family members in bereavement. But she is too young. See how many of her elegies are titled "On the Death of" some one. I wonder sometimes.

JOHN

What?

NATHANIEL

If her focus on death in these poems is an expression of her suppressed longing for freedom.

JOHN

We have raised her in the Christian faith, and there she finds solace.

NATHANIEL

No doubt, but some more recent poems express a linking of her longing for freedom with the cause.

JOHN

You refer to Sam Adams?

NATHANIEL

And John Hancock and others.

JOHN

There may be a few such references in some of her poems, but I don't think that will be fatal to her cause before the tribunal tomorrow.

NATHANIEL

This I know: Phillis writes from her heart. And she can't help seeing the oppression of the British troops on the people of Boston. She — more than any of us — understands what oppression is. And now she is beginning to understand something else.

Nathaniel turns away from the mirror to look directly at his father standing next to him.

JOHN

Understand what?

NATHANIEL

What freedom is.

JOHN

Is there something we have not given her?

NATHANIEL

Her manumission — her freedom. It is time, Father.

JOHN

Do you really think that Phillis would be better off if I granted her manumission tonight and threw her to the wolves? Do you think that if all the slaves in America were suddenly granted manumission, they would really be better off?

NATHANIEL

Yes.

(Pauses)

It would take time. But there can be no such thing as a happy slave, no matter how comfortable the cage. With respect to Phillis, there are no slaves in Boston, or in America, I wager ...

JOHN

(Cutting him off)

Wager not!

NATHANIEL

That are being put to the test that Phillis is. She hides it well, but when you think on it — we, in this family — have put so much pressure on Phillis to succeed, and now with this trial she must pass the test.

JOHN

I did not intend it this way – the trial was the idea of the publishers.

Suddenly exhausted, he crosses to the chair and sits down.

NATHANIEL

You know as well as I, Phillis is unlike the other Negro slaves of Boston. If something happened to you — to this family — what would become of her? Can you take away her education? Can you make her like the rest? Is Boston really ready for our Phillis?

JOHN

Is Phillis ready for Boston?

NATHANIEL

Don't you see what we have done? Through education we have freed her mind. Now it is time to free her body. Free her spirit.

JOHN

(Shaking his head)

Now I wonder if setting up this test that has now become a trial so that Phillis would have a chance to be published was such a good idea.

NATHANIEL

Do you now have doubts?

JOHN

This began as an elective, a choice, but now it has become something else. Phillis cannot fail tomorrow. Had I not arranged this, Phillis would be left alone happily writing her poetry. But now if she fails to prove she is the author before this group, she faces the prospect of being publically declared a charlatan, indeed a liar. As such she might as well be exiled for she will be a pariah in Boston. And what of this family? Your mother and I have been discussing Phillis's manumission for over a year, but there was always the question of how could she support herself.

NATHANIEL

Father, I was not aware of your and Mother's intentions regarding Phillis's manumission.

JOHN

Tomorrow the inquiry of Phillis will be presided over by Governor Thomas Hutchinson, the man who has been the target of so many vile onslaughts by the

"Sons of Liberty." And no one has more contempt for that organization — if I can call it that — than the lieutenant governor, who was hung in effigy, and had his house burned by them.

JOHN

Did you look at the scroll that was left on our doorstep this morning?

NATHANIEL

Let me see.

Crossing to the table, Nathaniel picks up the scroll tied with a scarlet ribbon and unrolls it, holding it before him with both hands.

NATHANIEL

It is a list of names.

JOHN

Read it to me, Nathaniel. It must be important, the manner of delivery.

NATHANIEL

(Reading)

"This is a true alphabetical list of the Sons of Liberty who dined under the Liberty Tree in Roxbury on July sixteenth, seventeen sixty-nine." It's a list of names.

JOHN

So, Nathaniel, is this list an attestation or a declaration?

NATHANIEL

It is a declaration. And I signed it at the bottom, just below Walsh.

(Pausing, pointing)

But that was almost three years ago. And at the bottom is a note reading "Be prepared for tomorrow – Oliver has a copy."

Stunned, John takes the scroll and reads with growing incomprehension.

JOHN

Oh, Nathaniel, how could you have signed the document. This is a great shock — especially this night - on the eve of the trial.

NATHANIEL

Father, it should come as no great surprise to you that many of my friends are Whigs. You and I have long disagreed on England's policy toward this colony.

JOHN

Associating with the Whigs is bad enough, but I did not know that you had declared that you are a "Son of Liberty." To dissent is one thing, but to put your name to something like this is quite another. You are quite right – it is a declaration – a declaration that you are an enemy of His Majesty's government.

NATHANIEL

Truly, Father, I declared I was a "Son of Liberty." And while I am discreet about it, yes I am one of that rabble — as you refer to them.

JOHN

I had no idea.

Dumbfounded, shaking his head.

NATHANIEL

But I can tell you that I would not have signed that document had I not believed in the cause.

JOHN

What cause?

NATHANIEL

The cause of freedom from the growing tyranny of the Crown and Parliament, and the King's lackeys here who regulate us under the oppressive edicts that emanate from these laws.

JOHN

These men — these so-called "Sons of Liberty." They are of the street. They pick a tree in Boston and hang the lieutenant governor in effigy there and call it a "Liberty Tree." They parade through the streets of Boston; they have secret codes. You are not like that! They would bring us all to destruction.

NATHANIEL

Andrew Oliver was the commissioner of customs when he was hung in effigy, and that was a protest against unjust customs duties – against the Stamp Act.

JOHN

No matter. He is the royal Lieutenant Governor. And we have to deal with him tomorrow, when he will be sitting in judgment on Phillis at the Common House.

NATHANIEL

You do not have to take my word for it. See, there are others who are respected and who have set their names to that list. You may be surprised. In fact, I can assure you that I will not be the only "Son of Liberty" to appear in the Common House tomorrow.

JOHN

At Phillis's trial?

NATHANIEL

Indeed, Father, on the jury itself. Regard the list.

JOHN

Why does everything having to do with the so-called "Sons of Liberty" have to be shrouded in such mystery, symbols, secret marks?

NATHANIEL

Freedom is not free; free men are not equal, and equal men are not free. Please, there is no mystery to a list of names.

John reads down the list.

JOHN

I will have to ponder that philosophy?

NATHANIEL

The H's, Father. See whose name is first under H.

JOHN

Don't tell me - John Hancock. Of course — I can see that. It is the only signature that is large enough for me to read. If you want to emulate someone on that list, emulate Mr. Hancock's penmanship.

NATHANIEL

But, Father, you may be missing the point.

JOHN

How so?

NATHANIEL

Has not Mr. John Hancock been invited to be part of this eminent group tomorrow?

JOHN

He has.

NATHANIEL

You see his name there?

JOHN

(Shaking his head)

Yes, I see his name, but still I have my doubts.

NATHANIEL

Why do you doubt that John Hancock is a "Son of Liberty"? He has been a selectman and town moderator. He has been at the forefront of supporting the more than one-century-old tradition of home rule for this city and this colony. And since the British began asserting ever more control over us, Hancock has been a major voice of dissent.

(Pausing)

Do you ever wonder why John Hancock's mansion — the finest in Boston — has been untouched by the mob? While that same mob has put the torch to the homes of Governor Hutchinson and Lieutenant Governor Oliver, and destroyed the property of other merchant shippers in Boston?

JOHN

I don't think on such things.

NATHANIEL

With due respect, perhaps you should.

JOHN

I do know what is whispered about Hancock among my friends.

NATHANIEL

What?

JOHN

That he is becoming Sam Adams's "milk cow."

NATHANIEL

Father, you are a staunch loyalist. Our home, this home, sits in the center of Boston, at the crossroads near the Common House, where the mob — as you call it — gathers to protest. Have you never feared that the mob would put this home to the torch?

JOHN

I have had those fears often, but I dared not share them with you.

NATHANIEL

Then I would ask you to contemplate that mystery.

JOHN

(Frustrated)

Enough of mysteries! There is no mystery in the fact that Phillis must stand before Governor Hutchinson, who will be the presiding judge tomorrow. I need not remind you of his unfailing loyalty to the King. And he apparently has a copy of your declaration.

CURTAIN

ACT TWO

Scene One

SCENE

The Governor's Council Chamber Room on the second level in the Common House.

TIME

Early the next morning, November 5, Guy Fawkes Day in England, celebrated as Pope's Day in Boston.

The room is simple, a set of French doors that rise to the high ceiling serve as a backdrop downstage. Flanking the French doors on either side are two large-pane glass windows that open on to a small balcony overlooking the head of King's Street. Upstage center, is a dais upon which is set a long judicial bench with two large chairs. Immediately next to the bench is a chair. There is a jury box and a small platformed stand for the accused. A counsels' table with chairs sits between the judicial bench and the jury box. The room is brightly lit from the chandelier.

AT RISE

Royal Governor Thomas Hutchinson and Lieutenant Governor Andrew Oliver of the Province of Massachusetts Bay Colony are together seated at the bench.

The wind-driven rain and sleet patter against the windows.

OLIVER

We risk life and limb coming into Boston, today of all days!

HUTCHINSON

My dear brother-in-law, this may be our last chance of restoring this city—indeed, this colony—to peace and loyalty to His Majesty. Carpe diem! We must seize every opportunity!

OLIVER

(Resignedly)

I expect the mob to start to gather below soon.

HUTCHINSON

I have been working on my opening address to the General Court when it reconvenes on January sixth.

OLIVER

Just two months hence — so soon.

HUTCHINSON

Indeed. Will you indulge me a moment of distraction from this attestation matter? I'd like your opinion.

OLIVER

Of course.

Looking down, Hutchinson clears his throat and reads aloud.

HUTCHINSON

"I have nothing in special command from His Majesty to lay before you at this time. That the government is at present in a disturbed and disordered state is a truth too evident to be denied. I am disappointed that I may not any longer, consistent with my duty to the King and my regard to the interest of the province, delay communicating my sentiments to you upon a matter of great importance."

OLIVER

It is true.

HUTCHINSON

And then I go on to recite the history of this colony and remind them of its foundation. "When our predecessors took possession of this colony under a grant and charter from the Crown of England, it was their sense, and it was the sense of the kingdom, that they were to remain subject to the supreme authority of Parliament."

OLIVER

And so it has been for over a century and a half.

HUTCHINSON

The theme is reconciliation, while at the same time holding true to our founding principles.

(Returning his attention to his speech)

"I have no desire, gentlemen, to do anything that I have laid to preclude you from seeking relief, in a constitutional way, in any causes in which you have heretofore or may hereafter support that you are aggrieved and, although I should not concur with you in sentiment. I will do nothing to lessen the weight which your representations deserve. I hope that we shall put an end to those irregularities which ever will be the portion of a government where the supreme authority is controverted and introduce the tranquility which seems to have taken place in most of the colonies upon this continent."

OLIVER

You are being most reasonable. Do you think this approach may succeed?

HUTCHINSON

The only alternative would be for them to break the bonds.

OLIVER

Resulting in anarchy and mob rule.

HUTCHINSON

We are in agreement.

(Pausing)

Now, let us talk of this Phillis's manuscript.

Oliver lays the manuscript before him.

OLIVER

I must say I would rather be almost anywhere than Boston on a day set aside for riots.

HUTCHINSON

The nor'easter favors us in this endeavor, and the sacrifice of being here this day is well worth it — if we can achieve our goal.

OLIVER

New evidence of treason abroad may come to light this day.

There is the sound of heavy footfalls from the steps below. Enter upstage a captain of the British Grenadier Guards dressed in full regalia. He approaches the royal governor and salutes.

CAPTAIN

Your Excellency, Governor Hutchinson, sir.

Hutchinson somewhat surprised.

HUTCHINSON

Captain, what brings you?

CAPTAIN

(To the lieutenant governor)

Your Excellency, Lieutenant Governor Oliver asked me to be here, sir.

OLIVER

Thank you for your presence this day, Captain.

CAPTAIN

The jurors are gathering below in the foyer.

OLIVER

Already? All of them?

CAPTAIN

Eleven, sir.

OLIVER

And Hancock?

CAPTAIN

Not yet, sir. This is the Nathaniel Wheatley document, sir.

The captain hands him a scroll.

OLIVER

(Taking the scroll)

Thank you, Captain. As soon as Hancock and the rest arrive, escort all of them up here to this chamber. Then, you and your men will proceed back to King's Street to serve this warrant, and escort the defendant back here.

(Hands him an envelope)

Finally, you and your men will assemble along the wall there and remain throughout the proceedings.

Oliver gestures toward the back of the courtroom.

CAPTAIN

Yes, sir.

The captain salutes and exits.

HUTCHINSON

(Surprised)

I thought that we had agreed that we would not need the guard today for this proceeding. I don't want another incident.

OLIVER

Nor do I. This precaution is to prevent exactly that. This missive handed me by the guard is a potential cause for riot.

HUTCHINSON

It's a narrow path we have to walk today. I do not want to politicize this trial.

OLIVER

Nor do I.

HUTCHINSON

I am not in total agreement that we should use the guard. I thought you understood. My plan for today is to try to take another step toward reconciliation with the Crown and these distinguished men who have many followers.

OLIVER

(Nervously)

But what of the mob! There are rumors that Mackintosh will lead them around the Common House. We must have protection in the Governor's Council Chamber.

HUTCHINSON

Andrew, agreeing to meet with the leaders of the town on a matter that is

not political in nature shows our good-
will toward this important group.

OLIVER

But we cannot escape politics — even
here, even this day. And this is the proof
that I needed.

(Oliver gleefully holds the scroll before him.)

HUTCHINSON

Proof? What is this?

OLIVER

For the Crown, it is a death warrant for
any and all who signed it.

HUTCHINSON

What?

OLIVER

This is the list of names of members of
the secret organization — the so-called
"Sons of Liberty." For years I have
sought to know who these instigators are
and now I do.

HUTCHINSON

The rabble that marches through the
streets intimidating those shop owners
and all who are loyal to the King?

OLIVER

The very same, who carry their signs and wear their secret symbols.

(Raising the list)

Now we know who they are.

HUTCHINSON

(Puzzled)

But what has this list to do with today's proceeding on the Wheatley slave, Phillis?

OLIVER

See near the bottom — one Nathaniel Wheatley has put his name thereto.

HUTCHINSON

The same one.

OLIVER

The very same — one of the family mentors for the defendant.

HUTCHINSON

I am still confused as to its relevance for today.

OLIVER

Don't you see? It establishes a linkage between the Wheatley family and the

"Sons of Liberty" and, by extension, this Phillis who is to be tested this day.

HUTCHINSON

Bringing this to light may not fit with my agenda this day.

OLIVER

Since the riots of the Stamp Act I have been the target of this group. Now is my chance to expose the lot of them.

HUTCHINSON

(Pausing)

I am reviled to this day because of the Stamp Act even after seven years since its passage.

OLIVER

Indeed.

HUTCHINSON

But over the past year we have served in office, we have striven mightily to restore a genuine loyalty to the Crown.

OLIVER

I know of no one in this colony who has served it more faithfully than you.

HUTCHINSON

You do know what will happen if we fail?

OLIVER

The King will likely appoint a military ruler for the Province of Massachusetts Bay Colony.

HUTCHINSON

And we could easily follow former Governor Bernard into exile in England. Then our only legacy will be to have been the last civilian Governor and Lieutenant Governor to preside over this Colony. Andrew, the better way is to reconcile where we can.

OLIVER

Would, say, a General Gage be any better, or have an easier time in ruling these stiff-necked Bostonians?

HUTCHINSON

These stiff-necked Bostonians, as you call them, are no different from you and me.

OLIVER

Except we remain loyal to the Crown! We are not like the firebrands who are so relentless in the pursuit of their traitorous objectives of spreading disunity.

HUTCHINSON

I meant to say we are like them in that we are Bostonians too. I say the majority of the people are loyal to the Crown. Be positive, man. Sam Adams and that mob are a vocal radical minority. If we can win over John Hancock to the moderate course of reconciliation, the rest will follow.

OLIVER

Yes, but how?

HUTCHINSON

John Hancock is a gentleman. Oh that we should be so popular with the people. I cannot imagine Hancock having anything to do with the "Sons of Liberty."

OLIVER

Yet, but his name appears on the list I showed you.

HUTCHINSON

So it does.

(Pausing)

That list is dated August of seventeen sixty-eight. Four years ago. Sometimes we all do foolish things.

OLIVER

You would deny me my day in court — my chance to expose those who hung me in effigy, those who led the mob that burned my home?

HUTCHINSON

I understand your humiliation at the hands of the mob, but this is not about you. I thought today we could perhaps take a step toward reconciliation. It would help garner support in the upcoming session of the General Court. Andrew, I don't have to remind you the Crown grows more impatient for results, and this day may offer us common ground with the political moderates.

OLIVER

How?

HUTCHINSON

The common ground I speak of lies in art, and poetry. Think on it.

OLIVER

(Lowering his voice conspiratorially)

Informants tell me that Hancock belongs to another, even more secretive organization called the "Loyal Nine."

HUTCHINSON

Another secret society?

OLIVER

According to my source, this is the policy-making group that directs its army, "the Sons of Liberty" like puppets.

HUTCHINSON

And they say Hancock belongs to this group?

OLIVER

Yes so it is whispered. These are the leaders who cannot be seen marching in the streets because they need to appear above the mob, perhaps even as being loyal. They direct this army of street brawlers. Mackintosh is their appointed General who imposes discipline and directs every move of every demonstration.

HUTCHINSON

What you say may be true, but, if so, why would John Hancock sign the declaration and why would he accept my commission as commander of the corps of cadets?

OLIVER

He can afford the best uniform, and he does like to play soldier.

HUTCHINSON

I am playing on his vanity of course, but are you suggesting that, even having accepted my commission, he could still covertly remain a member of these clandestine groups?

OLIVER

I don't know his motivations.

HUTCHINSON

This day I will proceed with my plan.

OLIVER

You believe it is not too late —even though they destroyed almost everything you had. Are they not beyond redemption?

HUTCHINSON

(Pauses, ignores the comment)

I am trying to look to the future, not the past. Just think on it, Andrew, if we can bring this most disobedient Province back to the proper service of His Majesty, then we will indeed have succeeded beyond all expectations. But time is critical. Things are relatively peaceful, commerce is improving with England, but this favorable wind could shift.

OLIVER

I am beginning to see how you are building your bridge.

HUTCHINSON

I have been generous. I have recently provided John Hancock with the two things he most desired: his commission as commander of cadets of the militia, and I have removed the ban on holding legislative sessions in Boston. I have decided to allow his precious legislature to return from their "exile" in Cambridge to resume meeting in Boston.

OLIVER

Now Mr. Hancock will only have to walk down past the Common from his mansion on Beacon Hill to attend the legislative sessions.

HUTCHINSON

Yes, Andrew. With his fortune and his ships plying the Atlantic between Boston and England, Johnny Hancock really has more in common with the Commercial Houses of Hutchinson and Oliver than with Sam Adams. And there's an added benefit. I believe that my allowing the legislature to return to Boston will please all the legislators, and they too will be more likely to compromise, to start to build their half of the bridge.

OLIVER

It certainly should. They have been constantly whining about the long trek over to Cambridge.

HUTCHINSON

In addition, these concessions might encourage them to morc readily authorize the payment of our salaries, although I expect that to change soon.

OLIVER

Oh, to be free of their control over our salaries, so that we could be paid regularly and without fear of our remuneration being delayed or cut off over policy differences.

HUTCHINSON

Soon we may be paid directly by the Royal Court.

OLIVER

(Surprised, with pleasant anticipation)

How could that be?

HUTCHINSON

(Lowering his voice)

Indeed, I am informed that in the not-too-distant future our salaries will be secure — this from a still-secret plan of the Crown.

OLIVER

What plan?

HUTCHINSON

A brilliant one.

(Pauses)

The plan is to impose a minuscule tax on tea coming into Boston Harbor.

Oliver leans back suddenly.

HUTCHINSON

(Surprised)

You do not seem as pleased as I would have expected.

OLIVER

I cannot help recall what happened when the Stamp Act tax was imposed and, as a result of it, I became the focus of their wrath.

HUTCHINSON

Things have changed since the days of the Stamp Act. I would not fear, Andrew. A small tax on tea would not cause much controversy.

OLIVER

(Pausing)

What a scandal it was for me and my family.

HUTCHINSON

(Becoming agitated)

You were not the only one, Andrew; my home was attacked by the mob, ransacked, my library of precious manuscripts trampled in the mud!

OLIVER

(Fatalistically)

In spite of that, you would reconcile with them?

HUTCHINSON

(Calming down)

What choice is there, other than that? I shudder to think. I am hoping and praying that those days are behind us. It is part of my plan that today's meeting will, I pray, begin the reconciliation.

OLIVER

(Fatalistically)

You will have my support in these new policies, as always, but I am not as strong as I once was, and my nerves have become affected. You know I had a breakdown just two years ago.

HUTCHINSON

But you have recovered now, and I have faith that you will be my strong right hand, as you always have been.

(Pauses)

Which brings us to the business at hand, this household slave. Have you read this manuscript?

Hutchinson picks up a sheaf of papers from the bench.

OLIVER

Yes.

HUTCHINSON

Is this poetry?

OLIVER

I am not a literary critic. We are here because any gathering of the most eminent men in Boston would have to include us. As far as I am concerned, to have this meeting is another expression

of our largess to the community. But
to answer your question, yes, I read it.
It is in my opinion not the sort of verse
one would expect of a slave. It is good,
very good. It is redolent of the rhymes of
Alexander Pope.

HUTCHINSON

I value your opinion, and I share it.

OLIVER

The question upon reading it is obvious.
Did this household slave write it? If
she did, it would be a most impressive
accomplishment.

HUTCHINSON

I agree that is the key question. Who
is to say that her mentors, Mary and
Nathaniel, did not write it?

OLIVER

And if we discover or have suspicions
that they did author, or helped author,
these poems, it raises the issue of perjury, and the legal consequences that
would follow.

HUTCHINSON

We — like the others — must decide
whether or not to sign the attestation.

As you suggest, we want to be sure of
the authenticity of her authorship before
we embarrass ourselves — and more
importantly, the Crown.

OLIVER

There is still another question regarding
this manuscript.

HUTCHINSON

And that is?

OLIVER

I detect one disturbing theme in some of
the poems in this manuscript.
(Picks it up from the bench)
Aside from the true authorship issue.

HUTCHINSON

That of?

OLIVER

Politics.

HUTCHINSON

Indeed?

OLIVER

A familiar name appears — a nemesis, I
might add.

HUTCHINSON

Who?

OLIVER

Americus!

HUTCHINSON

I did not make the connection when I read the manuscript.

OLIVER

The articles attributed to Americus that appear in the *Boston Gazette* are scurrilous in their criticism of the King and Parliament. It is rumored that Sam Adams writes these profanities under the pen name "Americus." My concern is that by using this name, is the author expressing through poetry the disturbing political philosophies of the "Sons of Liberty"?

HUTCHINSON

(Pondering the implications)

His Royal Highness would not be pleased to learn that we have signed an attestation for a poet who is subsequently found to be a fraud — or worse still, a revolutionary.

OLIVER

That is precisely my concern.

HUTCHINSON

So we must conduct the proceedings today as a trial in order to get to the truth of authorship and the question of the author's loyalty. To reach the truth we must have someone act as lead questioner. I would ask you to assume the role of chief cross-examiner this day.

OLIVER

It is an unsympathetic role. I share not her race or her status. The contrast is so stark. I am white, privileged, and rich, while she is but a poor black servant girl just ten years removed from Africa. The jury's sympathies will not lie with me. I will be seen as an oppressor. It will not add to my already sullied popularity.

HUTCHINSON

No, but it is another sacrifice I would ask of you. I want you to think of your role today as just that of a prosecutor on behalf of the Crown. Your duty is to probe her on these two issues: authenticity of authorship and loyalty. It might not add to your popularity here, but it will before the Royal Court. And it is the

only way to save us from being accused,
if later she is proven a fraud or disloyal,
of failing in our due diligence.

OLIVER

(Pausing, considering the options)

I agree. This group fomenting independence does not need another voice — especially a poet — a poet of their revolutionary behavior.

HUTCHINSON

But in your questioning, bear in mind that Hancock — and a few others on the jury, like the Reverend Samuel Cooper — may not share our intensity of loyalty to the Crown.

OLIVER

But we will have allies such as Mather Byles. I believe I can legitimately raise this theme of loyalty in my direct and cross-examinations. The reasons are obvious for the world to see.

HUTCHINSON

And remember – to serve our purposes, the attestation will have to be unanimous. All must sign.

OLIVER

A high bar, indeed. One that some would say is not attainable.

HUTCHINSON

And that could give us a way out. But still, we would not want to be the lone dissenters. We will wait and watch to see who will sign. If all do, then we will have no choice, otherwise we put ourselves in another unsympathetic position. Toward that end, is there someone here who you might call upon to question the defendant and perhaps call into doubt her literary claims?

OLIVER

Let me think on it.

HUTCHINSON

Perhaps one of our distinguished men of letters who will be here — a few of them are aspiring poets or writers themselves.

OLIVER

(Nodding)

Oh yes, a few of them are.

(Pausing)

I think I know the man to call.

HUTCHINSON

Who?

OLIVER

Joseph Green.

HUTCHINSON

Josey Green — the perfect choice —even
I have suffered under his satire.

(Pausing)

This is going to be a difficult proceeding.
We have already been exiles in our own
land; we do not want to end up like our
predecessor, Governor Bernard, as exiles
in London.

The captain enters and approaches the lieutenant governor.

CAPTAIN

Your Excellency, they have all assembled
— Hancock is there.

OLIVER

Send the jurors up first, so they can
assemble. Then separately, bring the
slave, Phillis, with her family.

The captain exits.

CURTAIN

ACT TWO

Scene Two

SCENE

The Governor's Council Chamber Room.

TIME

A few minutes later.

AT RISE

The last jurors are seating themselves in the jury box. They are followed by a Grenadier guard separating them from the Wheatleys: John, Susanna, Mary, Nathaniel, and finally, Phillis. A four-man guard forms up against the back wall. The Wheatleys, save Phillis, are directed to chairs at stage right. The single guard escorts Phillis to the small witness box. She enters and he closes the waist-high railing. She must stand facing the jury, for there is no chair. The Lieutenant Governor rises from counsel's table to face the jury. The guard crosses to form up with the other guards against the wall. Enter Governor Hutchinson, escorted by the bailiff/clerk of the court, to his chair at the high bench. Hutchinson takes his seat. The bailiff crosses to stand to the side of the bench. Hutchinson is wearing the scarlet robes of a chief justice of the Supreme Judicial Court. He is also wearing the traditional gray wig of the court.

BAILIFF/CLERK OF THE COURT

All stand. Hear ye, hear ye, the Supreme Judicial Court of the Province of

Massachusetts Bay Colony is now in
session. Governor Thomas Hutchinson
presiding. All ye having business before
this honorable court attend. God save
the King.

HUTCHINSON

(Looks around the room)

Be seated.

(Pauses; addresses the jury)

We are gathered in assembly here
today in solemn deliberation to determine whether or not one Miss Phillis
Wheatley,

(Gestures to the witness box)

household slave of John Wheatley of
Boston, who claims herself to be the
author of this manuscript of poems, "On
Subjects Religious and Moral," is indeed
the true and sole author of said manuscript. You have all had the opportunity
to read this manuscript, I trust?

He holds the manuscript in his hands and looks toward the jurors, who nod in assent.

HUTCHINSON

First, some words on the procedure that
I will follow today. It is my intention to
conduct this proceeding in a manner
as close to a regular trial as I am able

in order to determine the truth. This
concludes my opening remarks. Any
questions? Hearing none, now I believe
that Lieutenant Governor Oliver would
like to address you.

Oliver rises from counsel's table picks up a scroll and rolls it tight holding it in his right hand like a riding whip, and crosses to stand before the jury.

OLIVER

Today I ask you to think of me as a
prosecutor for the Crown in a search for
truth. During the course of this trial, I
will question closely the defendant

(Gestures to Phillis in the witness box)

and a few of those supporting her claim.

(Pauses)

This case comes to us from Mr.
John Wheatley, master of Phillis. As
background: you jurors should be
aware that the Susanna Wheatley, who
is mistress of the Wheatley household
and patron of Phillis, has over the course
of the last six months approached every
publisher in Boston requesting that
they publish this manuscript. All have
refused. And for one reason - that reason is doubt. Doubt that she

(points to the witness stand)

authored these poems. Now Mr. Wheatley has made a compact with the publishers that if the most prominent men in Boston, that is you, members of the jury, are willing to sign your names to an Attestation that having heard the evidence in open court, you believe Phillis to be the true and sole author of these poems, then the publishers will publish the manuscript along with the Attestation as a preface. You must remember that Mr. Wheatley's goal is one thing and that is for all of us to sign this Attestation.

Oliver crosses to counsels' table and picks up a sheet of foolscap and holds it up.

OLIVER

That is his goal. My goal and your goal, as members of the jury, is to test before we attest! Finally, for this Attestation to rise to the level to satisfy the purpose intended by the publishers, it must be signed by all jurors, the governor, and me, in our official capacity. Each of you may choose to sign if, after testing, you truly believe without reservation that Phillis here, not a dozen years hence from the barbaric wilds of Africa, is the true and sole author of this manuscript.

Any questions – hearing none, that concludes my opening remarks.

Oliver crosses back to counsel's table and sits in his chair.

The roar of the crowd outside on King's Street below brings the proceedings to a momentary halt. The bailiff rises, crosses downstage to the French doors, and looks down. He quickly crosses back to whisper in Hutchinson's ear.

HUTCHINSON

While I do not expect the gathering below to affect us in this room directly, I would urge that we move as expeditiously as possible to conclude these proceedings before the Pope's Day factions converge nearby for their annual melee. It is best we all be home safely before these events occur.

OLIVER

Thank you, Your Honor, I will finish as quickly as possible.

HUTCHINSON

Who speaks for the defendant?

JOHN

I do, Your Honor, John Wheatley.

John rises from his seat behind the defendant's and crosses to stand before the bench.

OLIVER

I object, Your Honor. John Wheatley is not an attorney, and he is conflicted as the owner of the slave in question.

HUTCHINSON

Mr. Wheatley we know you as a tailor, not an attorney.

JOHN

Yes, your Excellency. I did not believe that I would need to be an attorney. The truth will speak for itself.

HUTCHINSON

Mr. Wheatley, if the truth were so easy to obtain, we would not be here this day. As Mr. John Adams observed recently in another trial, "if men were angels. . . "

OLIVER

Mr. Wheatley, don't you see? The defendant is your property. The witnesses today will be your wife and your son. How can you cross-examine your own wife and son?

JOHN

But, Your Excellency, my family speaks the truth. Phillis speaks the truth.

OLIVER

I object, Your Honor, on the grounds of conflict of interest.

HUTCHINSON

The lieutenant governor is correct. I cannot allow this to go forward with you as the defendant's advocate.

JOHN

Governor, Your Honor, I have gone to so much effort. What about my son, Nathaniel?

OLIVER

Objection.

HUTCHINSON

It is the same problem. He has as many conflicts as you — maybe more.

He pauses, looking to the lieutenant governor, who slaps the scroll against his leg.

HUTCHINSON

We cannot proceed without a disinterested representative for the defendant.

At the very least, you need someone who
is not a member of the Wheatley family.

As Hutchinson looks around the room, John Hancock rises from the jury box.

HUTCHINSON

For what purposes does the gentleman rise?

HANCOCK

I am not an attorney, Your Excellency, but in order to prevent the abrupt termination of this hearing today without a resolution, I offer myself to serve as representative of the defendant.

OLIVER

Your Honor—

HUTCHINSON

Excuse me, Mr. Oliver, I am accommodating Mr. Wheatley by holding this proceeding. And I will accommodate Mr. Hancock's request.

OLIVER

I defer to the Chief Justice. It is his court.

HANCOCK

Indeed, I thought it was the people's court.

JURY

(Laughter)

HUTCHINSON

(Looking annoyed and frustrated)

Mr. Hancock, you will respect this court.

Hancock bows slightly and silently toward the bench.

HUTCHINSON

I see the Reverend Cooper would like to say something.

COOPER

It is appropriate that Mr. Hancock be allowed to represent the defendant, because I believe that Mr. Hancock has demonstrated by his actions the kind of selfless leadership in Boston that Moses exemplified in leading the Israelites out of bondage.

JURY

(Murmurs of assent and heads nodding in affirmation)

HUTCHINSON

Mr. Hancock, do you wish to make an opening statement?

HANCOCK

For obvious reasons, Governor, I have not prepared an opening statement. I beg the court's indulgence. However, I would like to say that the presence of the Grenadier Guards in this hallowed chamber seems inappropriate. Might I say intimidating.

JURY

(Murmurs of agreement, shaking of heads in affirmation, pounding of feet on the wooden floor)

HUTCHINSON

Why is their presence so offensive, to you, Mr. Hancock?

HANCOCK

For over a hundred and fifty years this colony has governed its own affairs and the Governor's Council has met in this very room. Now, so many changes have occurred over the past ten years that we find we are suddenly considered incapable of self-government. New and oppressive edicts emanate on a regular

basis limiting our time-honored liberty.
These laws, rules and regulations are an
affront to the people. Often each one
is a demand for additional tax revenue,
or restrictions on business. Isn't it bad
enough that our Town is now occupied
by British troops, but do we have to have
them in the courtroom as well?

JURY

(More murmurs of agreement, louder,
pounding of feet on the floor)

OLIVER

Your Honor, I object. This is not
relevant.

HUTCHINSON

(Addressing the captain)

Captain, you and your men are
dismissed.

The captain salutes, gives a muffled order, and the guards file smartly off, exiting the stage.

HUTCHINSON

Very well. You may call your first witness, Mr. Oliver.

Shaken by the rebuke, rattled, Oliver hesitates, trying to reorganize his thoughts.

OLIVER

Thank you, Your Honor. I – I call Susanna Wheatley.

Susanna rises nervously from her chair behind the defendant's box and crosses to the witness box next to the judicial bench. She stands as she is sworn-in by the bailiff.

OLIVER

State your name, please.

SUSANNA

Susanna Wheatley.

OLIVER

What is your address?

SUSANNA

We live at the corner of King's Street and Mackerel Lane. Just a block down King's Street from here.

She points toward the French doors.

OLIVER

Aside from you, who else resides at that residence?

SUSANNA

My husband, John, and Phillis. My daughter, Mary, Mrs. John Lathrop, and my son, Nathaniel, are frequent visitors.

OLIVER

Please describe your relationship to the defendant.

A huge roar is heard from the street below. The courtroom turns silent in anticipation.

OLIVER

(Nervously)

What is that disturbance?

HANCOCK

It is the cheer from the people as the guard is seen exiting the building to King's Street below.

HUTCHINSON

Mr. Oliver, in the interest of time, and to help in your laying a foundation, the court takes judicial notice that Susanna Wheatley rescued the defendant when she was approximately seven years old from a brig, the *Phillis*, at Beach Street wharf in Boston eleven years ago. The family named Phillis after the brig that brought her, and ever since the defendant has resided with, and served as a household servant to the Wheatley family,

(Gesturing)

who have all been involved in mentoring her up to the present time.

SUSANNA

And within eighteen months of tutoring from my daughter, Mary, especially, and Nathaniel, our little Phillis was reading even the most difficult passages in the Bible. And she was writing.

OLIVER

Do you believe that she comprehended what she read? Or was she just mouthing the words like some exotic bird — say, an African parrot.

HANCOCK

I object, Your Honor, to this gratuitously disparaging remark.

HUTCHINSON

It may be relevant. After all, the issue before us is imitation, is it not? And isn't that what parrots do?

SUSANNA

It was clear to us that Phillis understood what she was reading, and the more she read, the more she understood. It was then that I became convinced that this was no ordinary child, but a child prodigy.

OLIVER

A child prodigy?

SUSANNA

Yes. A gifted child.

OLIVER

A gifted child.

(Pausing)

That is all the questions I have for Susanna Wheatley.

HUTCHINSON

Mr. Hancock, have you a question for the witness?

HANCOCK

Only a comment your Honor.

HUTCHINSON

Allowed.

HANCOCK

Mr. Oliver seems perplexed that Phillis could be a child prodigy. Indeed, that such children exist at all. Am I correct, Mr. Oliver?

OLIVER

Mr. Hancock, I have never seen a child prodigy — have you?

HANCOCK

I had the honor of attending the Boston Latin School several years after Mr. Benjamin Franklin, whose record there no one has matched. And we all know of his amazing accomplishments.

(To Hutchinson)

Thank you, your grace.

HUTCHINSON

Proceed, please, Mr. Oliver.

OLIVER

Thank you, Your Honor.

HUTCHINSON

Mr. Hancock? His Excellency, the Lieutenant Governor, has it correct. In this proceeding, please address me as "Your Honor." For here I appear as the chief justice of the Supreme Judicial

Court, not as Governor of the Province of Massachusetts Bay Colony.

HANCOCK

Of course, Your Honor, but you raise an important procedural issue. Do you think it a wise precept when two of the most important offices of government are combined in the same individual?

HUTCHINSON

I did not seek this this honor on myself, I was chosen.

HANCOCK

Do you not see the folly? As Montesquieu said in his book *The Spirit of the Laws*, "when the legislative and executive powers are united in the same person or body, there can be no liberty."

HUTCHINSON

I am not on trial here.

HANCOCK

I am afraid we all are.

HUTCHINSON

Indeed, Mr. Hancock, you may differ, but I am doing my duty as I see it.

Mr. Oliver, do you have any further
questions of this witness?

OLIVER

No, your Honor.

HUTCHINSON

You are dismissed, Mrs. Wheatley, but
do not leave the courtroom, as we may
need to call upon you again.

Susanna, somewhat shaken, rises and crosses to return to her seat behind the defendant's box.

OLIVER

I call the defendant, Phillis, household
slave of John and Susanna Wheatley.

The lieutenant governor crosses to the defendant's box with a Bible in hand.

OLIVER

Put your left hand on the Bible and
raise your right hand. Do you swear by
Almighty God to tell the whole truth?

PHILLIS

I do.

HUTCHINSON

Would you like to make a statement
before we begin the questioning?

Suddenly, Phillis falls to her knees in the defendant's box, and, placing her hands together in a prayerful position on the railing before her, slowly lifts her eyes heavenward.

PHILLIS

"Arise, my soul, on wings enraptur'd,
rise to praise the monarch of the earth
and skies."

JURY

(Murmurs)

HUTCHINSON

What is this?

Susanna quickly leaves her seat behind Phillis and crosses to the witness box. She bends over the rail and reaches in, as if to lift Phillis.

OLIVER

You there! Return to your seat. There
will be no coaching of the defendant.

Susanna stands and crosses back.

OLIVER

I object to these actions, and irrelevant prayers and parables.

HUTCHINSON

Order. Order. I direct the witness to stand and to answer all questions forthrightly.

HANCOCK

I beg Your Honor's indulgence. I believe the witness — ah, in Your Honor's words, the defendant's —statement may be appropriate and relevant.

OLIVER

Mr. Hancock!

Hancock crosses to counsel's table, retrieves the manuscript, and crosses to face the jury.

HANCOCK

Our purpose here today is to sign an Attestation as to whether we believe the witness is the author of this manuscript. Is that not true?

HUTCHINSON

Yes, of course.

Hancock shuffles through the pages of the manuscript.

HANCOCK

I did have the opportunity to read this manuscript and I believe that ... yes, here it is. Phillis has recited the beginning of her poem entitled: "Thoughts on Works of Providence." Surely the fact that she recites her own poetry is relevant.

OLIVER

Objection. The defendant may have the capacity to memorize a poem, but that does not prove she is the true author. As I plan to show later, another member of the Wheatley family may have authored this manuscript. Or, Mr. Hancock, have you already reached a conclusion on this as well — the ultimate issue before us today?

HUTCHINSON

The Lieutenant Governor's objection is well taken. Please keep in mind, Mr. Hancock, the truths we need to establish this day. And the burden of proving that is upon the defendant.

HANCOCK

Allow me to assure the Lieutenant Governor that I will not put my name to any attestation unless I truly believe that Phillis is the true and only author of these poems.

OLIVER

Governor, Your Honor, I would like to proceed with the Crown's case.

HUTCHINSON

Proceed, Mr. Prosecutor.

OLIVER

Your Honor has graciously consented to allow members of the jury to question the defendant. Does any member of the jury have questions? I recognize the Reverend Mather Byles.

BYLES

May I approach the witness, Your Honor?

HUTCHINSON

You may approach the defendant.

Byles exits the jury box and crosses to the defendant's stand approaching slowly, as if in anticipation of examining some exotic creature.

BYLES

Oh yes, indeed. Now, may I call you Phillis?

PHILLIS

(Coughing)
Please, sir.

BYLES

Phillis, what is a muse?

PHILLIS

It is an allusion, sir—

OLIVER

I object to these irrelevant references to allusions.

BYLES

No, no, no, Sir. A muse is very important to a poet. Being the poet I am, I know.

HUTCHINSON

(Frustrated)
Reverend Byles, do you have a question?

BYLES

Yes, ah, here it is. Phillis, who is this Maecenas?

PHILLIS

Maecenas, sir, he is one of my muses.

HUTCHINSON

(Pounding the gavel)

Order. Order. I direct the defendant to answer the question directly.

PHILLIS

Gaius Maecenas was the Roman statesman and patron of the arts who helped Horace, Virgil, and Terence — the Roman poets.

OLIVER

A Roman poet named Terence?

PHILLIS

Yes, Your Excellency, Terence was a great Roman poet — and, like me, from Africa.

BYLES

She's right, Mr. Prosecutor, she knows her Roman history.

OLIVER

It is a triviality.

HANCOCK

Objection, Your Honor, the fact that she can teach our learned prosecutor something of classical literature goes directly to the point of her being capable of writing this manuscript.

BYLES

Oh, Mr. Hancock is correct indeed—you do know your classics.

(Addressing Phillis)

That is good, very good. But tell me, Phillis, do you have any living poet as a muse?

PHILLIS

Dear Sir, I have many.

BYLES

(Sensing her anxiety)

Excuse me for interrupting, but to put you at your ease, I want you to know that my muse was my cat.

(Momentarily lowering his eyes, looking sad).

And since she died my poetic voice is stilled.

PHILLIS

Dear Reverend Byles, I am sorry for your cat. What was her name?

BYLES

I called her Muse.

PHILLIS

What kind of cat was she?

BYLES

Oh, she was a big yellow Calico. And thank you for asking.

Oliver looks toward the bench with frustration and raises his hands, palms upward, as a gesture of futility in controlling his witness.

OLIVER

I am sorry, Your Honor, I have to object to this line of irrelevant questions.

BYLES

Yes, your Honor.

Turning back to Phillis, Byles fidgets with the manuscript in his hands.

BYLES

Now, Phillis, I am going to put you to a little test. I am going to recite a poem and I want you to answer two questions. Who is the author? And who is the subject? Do you understand?

PHILLIS

Yes, sir.

BYLES

"When I attend to his immortal lyre, I kindle instant with a sacred fire; now here, now there, my soul pursues his song, hurried impetuous by his pow'r along."

PHILLIS

Oh, sir, the poem is one written by yourself.

BYLES

(Taken aback, smiling broadly)

Very well done. Let me ask you, since you know the poem: you also know its subject matter?

PHILLIS

Sir, you are expressing how you feel when you read the poetry of Alexander Pope.

BYLES

How do you know that?

PHILLIS

Because it is the same way I feel, but ne'er was able to express so well.

BYLES

Oh my. Wonderful. I am flabbergasted — no, delighted —overwhelmed. May you never lose your Muse. I have concluded my questions, Mr. Prosecutor.

HANCOCK

May I question Reverend Byles?

OLIVER

(Looking a bit perturbed)

Most irregular.

HUTCHINSON

I will allow it.

HANCOCK

Now - we all know now that your muse was your cat.

JURY

(Laughter)

HANCOCK

So you have testified that you named your cat thus.

BYLES

Indeed I did, and I greatly lament her passing. It has left me silent. The source

of my inspiration purrs no more. And so
now I am dulled.

HANCOCK

And when not even Muse's purring
could give sustenance, did you not say,
"Oft to the well-known volumes have
I gone and stole a line from Pope or
Addison."

BYLES

Ah yes, an oft-quoted phrase among
poets. We poets all need inspiration.
And what better inspiration is there than
the greatest poets of the day. Not, of
course, to suggest that I am a great poet.

Byles bows in modesty.

OLIVER

Thank you, Mr. Byles.
(To the jury)
You can imitate someone's style, but
themes — I don't think so easily.
(Turning from the jury to face the bench)
Your Honor, I believe that the eminent
satirist and essayist, Mr. Joseph Green,
who graces us with his presence today,
would like to pose some questions to the
defendant.

HUTCHINSON

Please call Mr. Green.

Joseph Green leaves the jury box and crosses to the bench. He is holding in his right hand a copy of a broadsheet newspaper and the manuscript.

Green is sworn.

GREEN

Yes, thank you, your Honor,
Mr. Prosecutor.

OLIVER

Mr. Green, would you kindly identify
your literary credentials for the jury.

Green crosses to stand before the jury.

GREEN

Good morning. As some in this room
may know, I am Joseph Green. I travel
to England with some frequency,
where I am perhaps better known in
the literary circles there. I am in fact a
scholar of poetry. I have even tried my
hand at it, with some modest success. I
count among my acquaintances the late
Alexander Pope. I have written and published literary criticism in England and
America.

OLIVER

Any question to Mr. Green on his credentials?

(Pauses)

Hearing none, I will now ask Mr. Green to question the witness.

Green crosses to Phillis to stand before her. She begins to cough.

PHILLIS

Good morning, sir.

GREEN

Phillis, do you know me?

PHILLIS

No, sir, I do not know you - other than you are a most eminent man.

GREEN

Thank you for saying that, although some — even in this room — may not agree with you.

There is the sound of muffled laughter.

GREEN

Allow me to say that I am somewhat of a scholar of English literature. I am a great admirer of Jonathan Swift,

John Donne, and John Milton, besides Alexander Pope, to name a few.

(Pauses)

I have some questions to put to you this day.

PHILLIS

Yes, sir, of course. That is my purpose this day.

GREEN

Tell me, Phillis, do you remember your family life on the Windward Coast?

PHILLIS

(Taken aback momentarily, coughing)

I remember very little, sir. There is one thing. I can picture my mother pouring water out of a jar at sunrise. It was a ceremony — a form of worship of the sun — of that I am sure.

GREEN

Have you written of this time in your life there?

PHILLIS

A few lines, sir.

GREEN

Would you recite it, please?

PHILLIS

(Pausing)

"Ah, what bitter Pangs molest — what sorrows labored in the parent breast? That, more than stone, ne'er soft compassion moved who from its father seized his much beloved."

GREEN

Good. Tell me, please, Phillis, have you read any of these authors that I mentioned?

PHILLIS

Oh yes, sir.

GREEN

Which one?

PHILLIS

Sir, I have read them all.

GREEN

All? Pray, tell me what it is you like about all these authors.

PHILLIS

(Coughing)

Excuse me, sir.

GREEN

That is all right. You may take your time. Would you like a glass of water?

PHILLIS

Oh, yes, sir.

Susanna Wheatley exits.

GREEN

Are you feeling well enough to resume?

PHILLIS

Yes, sir.

GREEN

What is it that you most admire about John Milton?

PHILLIS

Reverend Byles, John Milton's greatest work is *Paradise Lost*.

GREEN

You are correct in pointing out that John Milton is most famous for his poem entitled *Paradise Lost*, which is a paean in praise of God. Do you think that an atheist would be as enamored of Mr. Milton's poetry as you are?

PHILLIS

I do not know, sir.

GREEN

What are your views on atheists?

PHILLIS

I have written a poem about atheists.

GREEN

By all means, please recite from it.

PHILLIS

"If there's no god from whence did all
things spring?
He made the greatest and minutest
thing if there's no heaven whither wilt
thou go make thy Elysium in the shades
below."

JURY

(Murmurs of assent and approval)

ELLIOT

(Rising in jury box)

I have never heard a better expression of
the error of atheism.

HUTCHINSON

(Banging the gavel)

Order, order.

GREEN

(To Phillis)

Are you aware that your work bears
a striking resemblance to the work of
Alexander Pope?

PHILLIS

He is my favorite author.

GREEN

Indeed, he must be — for some would
say that in your work there is too
much Pope and not enough Wheatley.
Rhymes, doesn't it, like a couplet?

JURY

(Moans)

PHILLIS

I am not sure that I understand, sir.

GREEN

Allow me to begin again. The issue at
hand is not whether your work is imita-
tive, but rather whether your work is
indeed your work. You see, we in this
room have never beheld a creation such
as yourself – so well schooled in every
grace.

PHILLIS

You mean of my race?

GREEN

You must understand you are the first of African descent that we have seen who lays claims to write poetry.

Green crosses to counsel's table, places the manuscript and broadsheet on it, and crosses back to stand before Phillis.

GREEN

No - more than that - a household slave who claims to write poetry like the great poets of English literature.

PHILLIS

Please, Mr. Green, I must correct you. Ever since my mistress took me to her home, I have not been treated like a slave, nor even like a servant. No, quite the contrary, I have been treated like a member of the Wheatley family, as a daughter and a sister. They taught me to read and write. The Wheatleys have provided me with my own room where I can write. Mary tutored me.

GREEN

(Surprised)

You are fortunate indeed. I doubt if any other household slave in Boston has her own room in her master's home.

PHILLIS

And my mistress has graciously provided me candles and a fireplace. If my muse comes to me at night, I can write what she tells me, lest I forget.

GREEN

(Pausing)

And so now you have ventured forth and you sit amidst strangers. If we approve of your authorship of this manuscript, you will be the first published woman of African descent. You may become famous and rich.

Green crosses to counsel's table to retrieve the manuscript and broadsheet, and returns to stand before the jury, still addressing Phillis.

GREEN

The world will know that you come from our Town. Therefore, it is necessary that we citizens of Boston protect ourselves from the skepticism that will no doubt greet this book,

(Holding the manuscript high, addressing the jury)

if it ever becomes a published work. The
only way we can do this is to be abso-
lutely sure that the defendant is the
author. Otherwise, we will be party to a
fraud: a fraud that would be a disgrace to
the people of Boston, a disgrace to you,
(Addressing the defendant)
a disgrace to the Wheatley family, and, I
might add, a disgrace particularly to us
the jury of this honorable court.

HANCOCK
I object to this intimidation of the
defendant. Mr. Green's hysterics are
prejudicial. The jury would think
that the safer way is not to sign the
Attestation.

Elliot rises.

HUTCHINSON
Reverend Elliot?

ELLIOT
Your Honor, like so many of this day
who consider themselves enlightened by
valuing reason over faith, Mr. Green's
artful addresses pander to base passions,
and instill fear of the consequences of
signing the Attestation. As for me, such
speeches lead people to metaphysical
jargon, to folly, to madness, but not to
the truth.

JURY

(Murmurs of assent)

HUTCHINSON

Order, order.

GREEN

Your Honor, I have other questions.

HUTCHINSON

Proceed, Mr. Green, with your questions.

Green crosses back to stand before Phillis.

GREEN

Let me probe the defendant's knowledge of the greatest poet of the English language. Who might that be?

PHILLIS

(Anticipating the question)

It is to me John Milton, sir?

GREEN

Not William Shakespeare? I am surprised. Of course, Milton, can be your choice. But most in this room could recite a passage or two from Milton and or Shakespeare if called upon. Milton is your choice then. Which means to me that you have prepared yourself to recite his poetry. That is fine. But to be fair I will not ask you to recite another passage but rather query you on another aspect of the poet. There was in his life something that caused him great distress. Do you know what that might have been?

PHILLIS

"When I consider how my light is spent ere half my days in this dark world and wide. . ."

GREEN

(Mildly surprised)

"On his blindness," very good. You have proven that you have memorized some Milton. Now, I am going to recite a passage, and when you know who wrote this passage, please raise your hand. I will stop reading and you can tell us who the author is. Do you understand?

PHILLIS

Yes, I understand, I will try, sir.

GREEN

"Hail, happy day, when, smiling like the morn - "

Phillis raises her hand.

GREEN

"Fair freedom rose New England to adorn." You know the author?

PHILLIS

How could I not, sir? It is my very own humble work.

GREEN

From which poem, may I ask?

PHILLIS

My poem entitled "To the Right Honorable William, Earl of Dartmouth, His Majesty's Principal Secretary of State for North America."

Green looks down at the manuscript he holds in his hand.

GREEN

Indeed. Now, I want to ask you a question about the substance of this poem. Explain the use of the words "fair freedom."

PHILLIS

Sir, do you mean, what is fair freedom?

GREEN

Exactly.

PHILLIS

Fair freedom is best explained in metaphor and simile.

OLIVER

(Frustrated)

I object to these literary terms. Metaphor and simile! Allusions and illusions!

GREEN

Please, Governor, if I may be allowed to continue to plow this field of inquiry, I believe it will have a rich harvest.

HUTCHINSON

Mr. Oliver has a point. Proceed. But I direct the defendant to speak in concrete terms that we all understand. Some of us may not be as schooled or gifted in this art as she.

GREEN

Please continue, Phillis — you were going to explain what you meant by "fair freedom."

PHILLIS

Yes, sir. "Fair freedom." What I meant...

(Pausing, looking up to the ceiling)

It is like the air we breathe. Without it we suffocate. "Fair freedom" is liberty's twin. And virtue is the mother of liberty.

GREEN

More metaphors and similes - "Fair freedom" can mean many things to many people. And the same can be said for "liberty" and "virtue." For example, some may read a political message here. Do you understand what I mean by a political message?

PHILLIS

I am not sure, sir.

GREEN

Well, suppose His Majesty's new ambassador, Lord North, were to read your poem. Might he not reasonably conclude that this is a comment on the conduct and policies of his office?

PHILLIS

I am not sure I did not mean...

GREEN

I am sure that you — as an intelligent and educated young woman — are aware of some of these new philosophies that are abroad.

PHILLIS

You mean the atheists?

JURY

(Laughter)

Green gestures toward the French doors.

GREEN

No, you need not look so far afield. I refer to some of the philosophers of the streets of Boston. Recently I came across a passage by one of these philosophers. I will read it, and I would like you to tell me who wrote it.

PHILLIS

(Coughing)

Yes, sir.

Green raises the copy of the *Boston Gazette*, holding it high, and pirouettes slowly to show it to the jury, the prosecutor, and the judge. Then, facing Phillis, he looks down at the broadsheet.

GREEN

"I am forced to get my living by my brow, as most of you are. But I pledge to you I will continue to defy those in power, those who owe their grandeur and honors to grinding the faces of the poor and schooled in the arts of ill-gotten gain and power."

PHILLIS

(Coughing)

I have no idea who the author is, sir. I am sorry.

GREEN

The author is one James Otis. This is what I mean by the new philosophers. You find their words most often published in the *Boston Gazette* that spews forth from the radical Whigs of Boston.

PHILLIS

I am sorry, sir.

HANCOCK

Your Honor, objection, the questioner should confine his line of inquiry to poetry, not inquire on political philosophy. The defendant claims to be a poet, not a politician. She is on trial for her poetry, not her politics.

HUTCHINSON

I will allow this line of questions. We are here to get at the truth of the matter, and if it takes probing into the politics of the defendant, then so be it.

GREEN

Thank you, Your Honor.

(Turning to face the jury, his back to Phillis)

Gentlemen, one need only to go to the wharves and ropewalks and taverns on any Monday morning after the *Gazette* has been published. Then you will hear them quoting another poet — another philosopher: one so-called "Americus."

(Turning to confront Phillis)

And tell us, please — who is this "Americus"?

PHILLIS

"Americus"?

GREEN

Indeed, does the name not sound familiar to you? Certainly one who can teach us of Gaius Maecenas should have no trouble remembering "Americus." Certainly you know of these radical Whigs who fashion themselves as latter-day Romans, and this "Americus" is always spouting like a Roman fountain about the latest perceived injustice of the British troops, or some new oppression by the British Parliament against America. You know Americus, do you not?

PHILLIS

(Coughing)

Sir, I mentioned the name in a poem.

GREEN

In seventeen sixty-eight, to be precise.

PHILLIS

Yes.

GREEN

Now, let me read something to you and you tell me the author's name.

PHILLIS

Yes, sir.

GREEN

"A certain lady had an only son he grew up daily virtuous as he grew, fearing his strength which she undoubted knew; she laid some taxes on her darling son."

PHILLIS

Sir?

GREEN

"And would have laid another act there on; amend your manners I'll the taxes remove; was said with seeming

sympathy and love by many scourges
she his goodness tried until at length the
best of infants cried he wept, Britannia
turned a senseless ear"

PHILLIS

(Coughing)
Sir?

GREEN

"At last awakened by maternal fear why
weeps Americus why weeps my Child.
Thus spake Britannia, thus benign and
mild." Does this sound familiar?

PHILLIS

It is mine, sir.

GREEN

Allow me to continue, please. "He weeps
afresh to feel his iron chain turn, Oh
Britannia claim thy child again." And so
on. When was this polemic —

HANCOCK

Objection, Your Honor!

HUTCHINSON

Mr. Green, please rephrase your
question.

GREEN

When was this poem written?

HANCOCK

Objection!

HUTCHINSON

State the nature of your objection.

HANCOCK

Mr. Green presumes that Phillis is copying the *Boston Gazette* in the use of the term "Americus." I submit that he has it backwards. The *Boston Gazette* is using a term first coined by the defendant.

GREEN

The sentiment is the same, no matter.

HANCOCK

Not quite. Certainly, gentlemen of the jury, we recognize in this poem the symbol of the chain. You must understand that the defendant that stands before us was as a small child chained like an animal during a march to a slave factor in Africa, and then transferred to a ship on the windward coast. She may have been chained some of the time while on board the ship that brought her here. She has felt the metal manacles on her wrists and ankles. The chain — this terrible memory —is so much a part of her that it is her imagery throughout her poetry. Indeed, it is a theme, a symbol, that sets her poetry apart from that of Mr. Pope, Mr. Donne, and Mr. Milton, and all the rest.

GREEN

(Gesturing)

Granted.

PHILLIS

I have forgotten.

GREEN

But to rephrase my earlier question, wherein Mr. Hancock asserted that the *Boston Gazette* copied you in using the term Americus ...

PHILLIS

(As if to herself)

But I remember the advertisements.

GREEN

(Surprised, turning to face Phillis)

What advertisements?

PHILLIS

Do you want me to recite one?

GREEN

No!

OLIVER

I do not see the relevance!

HANCOCK

Your Honor, Mr. Green has opened this line of inquiry. I think it only fair to allow the defendant to complete her answer.

HUTCHINSON

The defendant may continue her answer.

PHILLIS

(Addressing the jury)

"To be sold, a parcel of likely Negroes, imported from Africa, cheap for sale or short credit with interest, inquire of John Avery, at his House next door to the White Wharf, or his store adjoining. Also if any person have any Negro men strong and heavy, though not of the best moral character, may have an exchange for small Negroes."

GREEN

What is your point?

PHILLIS

Only one, sir, the Americus I wrote of would not espouse that philosophy! I wrote: "But how, presumptuous shall we hope to find Divine acceptance with the Almighty mind while yet (Oh, deed ungenerous) they disgrace and hold in bondage Afric's blameless race? Let virtue reign — and thou accord our prayers be victory ours and generous freedom theirs."

JURY

(Murmurs of assent)

GREEN

(Momentarily taken aback)

I see. Hmm. Ah, let's return to your homage to the Honorable Lord Dartmouth. When you wrote the poem, did you believe that Lord Dartmouth might actually see it and read it?

PHILLIS

Sir, I was presumptuous. But God works in mysterious ways his wonders to reveal. Who would have ever dreamt that I would someday be in a position to address such an august body of men as you? Yet, I see a great opportunity for Lord Dartmouth. Sir, may I quote my poem?

GREEN

You may.

PHILLIS

"No more, America, in mournful strain
of wrongs, and grievance unredress'd
complain, thou dread the iron chain,
which wanton tyranny with lawless hand
had made, and with it meant' enslave
the land."

GREEN

(Addressing the jury)

You have heard it. Out of her lips.

(Turning back to Phillis)

Precisely, to what wrongs and grievances do you refer?

PHILLIS

Oh, sir, the heavy burdens laid upon our beloved Town.

GREEN

Can you be specific as to these burdens?

PHILLIS

I know them well!

HANCOCK

As does everyone in Boston!

HUTCHINSON

Mr. Hancock, let her answer! You are not on trial.

OLIVER

(Inserting)

Yet.

GREEN

(To Phillis)

Please share this with me, with the court, and with the jury — what burdens on Boston?

PHILLIS

Sir, it began with the Writs of Assistance, followed by the Stamp Act, the Townsend Acts, the murder of the young Snyder boy — who lived but a few blocks away. It continues with the quartering of British troops in our neighborhoods and homes. And to the bloody Boston Massacre which took place just two years ago on King's Street below.

Phillis gestures toward the French doors.

GREEN

How is it that these things are so important to you?

PHILLIS

Sir, some occurred practically on the doorstep of the Wheatley mansion. I have witnessed — as have all of us — these events or their results on our Town.

JURY

(Murmurs of assent)

GREEN

(Pausing, looking down at the manuscript)

You must be patient; you come to us, at least to me, as a surprise revelation. Quite frankly, like many of my colleagues, I look at you and I see a young household slave girl. Yet, when I hear your elegant speech and poetry - I am puzzled, if not befuddled.

PHILLIS

(Coughing)

At home, with my family, I am Phillis. Here, I am a freak.

GREEN

(Warming to Phillis)

No, no, my dear child, you are not a freak. But why do you persist in this passion — this theme — of Boston being held in bondage? I am sure that many in this room find this subject matter not appropriate for poetry.

(Pleading)

Why not just concentrate on your elegies on morality and theology, on things not of this world?

PHILLIS

(Coughing)

I am what I am. I cannot be what I perceive others may want me to be.

HANCOCK

If you permit me, your Honor.

HUTCHINSON

Yes, Mr. Hancock.

HANCOCK

This young woman who stands before us has actually felt the manacles and chains of bondage. She has borne the horrors of the "Middle Passage." These experiences obviously would affect her political philosophy and her poetry.

OLIVER

Yet again, Mr. Hancock tries to turn the issue from finding the truth. During my questioning, she

(Gesturing to Phillis)

exhibited little memory of her past life in that continent.

HUTCHINSON

Let the defendant answer.

PHILLIS

Please, I am sorry, Your Honor. What is the question?

Green turns from counsel's table to where Hancock stands, to face Phillis.

GREEN

If I may rephrase the question, it is Mr. Hancock's contention that your having been captured by slavers in Africa has given you an insight into this so-called "tyranny" of which you wrote in your poem to Lord Dartmouth.

PHILLIS

Only that I thought the appointment of Lord Dartmouth would be good for Boston and good for this province, this colony and America. Such was my hope. And if it were so, then it would be good for His Majesty the King.

HANCOCK

Your Honor, if I may? I have a few more questions.

OLIVER

I object.

JURY

(Murmurs of discontent with Oliver's objection)

HANCOCK

Your Honor, Mr. Prosecutor does not know what I am about to say.

HUTCHINSON

Proceed, Mr. Hancock.

Hancock crosses to stands near his chair at counsel's table and addresses the jury.

HANCOCK

While politics, and religion to some degree, may divide us in this room, there are more things that we are united upon. I doubt that anyone here today could argue that the policies of His Majesty's government toward this province do not need improvement. Phillis is merely articulating in her poetry what we all know to be fact.

OLIVER

Objection!

GREEN

(Turning from Hancock to address Phillis)

So, to return to my question, you have felt compelled to memorialize these political sentiments in your poetry?

PHILLIS

Yes, Mr. Green, sir.

GREEN

So, do you mind if I elaborate a little more from your poetry?

PHILLIS

No, sir.

GREEN

You write further on in the poem: "America need no longer dread the iron chain, which wanton tyranny with lawless hand had made, and with it meant to enslave the land."

Reverend Elliot rises in the jury box.

HUTCHINSON

I recognize the Reverend Elliot.

ELLIOT

All power has its foundation in compact and mutual consent, or else it proceeds from fraud or violence.

JURY

(Loud noises of assent)

OLIVER

(Turning to Phillis)

To me, your poem smacks of demagoguery. Indeed, it sounds not so much of Pope, but rather of Sam Adams.

JURY

(Louder noises of disagreement)

HUTCHINSON

(Pounding his gavel)

Order, order.

PHILLIS

(To Oliver)

Forgive me, sir, I did not mean it as you describe.

GREEN

Are you alleging in this poem that Britain would enslave us all here in the Province of Massachusetts Bay Colony?

HANCOCK

Your Honor.

HUTCHINSON

(Frustrated)

What now, Mr. Hancock?

OLIVER

Governor, you must direct the defendant to answer Mr. Green's question.

HANCOCK

Your Honor, I would like Mr. Green to ask her to recall further in that same poem what she has written.

HUTCHINSON

Mr. Green, do you have any objections?

GREEN

No, your Honor.

HANCOCK

(To Phillis)

In that poem addressing Lord Dartmouth, please recite what you wrote beginning with: "You my lord may well wonder."

PHILLIS

(Pausing)

"You my lord may well wonder, whence such daring boldness sprung, whence flow my wishes for the common good, by feeling hearts alone best understood?
From native clime, when seeming cruel fate me snatch'd from Afric's fancied happy seat, impetuous — ah what bitter pangs molest, what sorrows laboured in the parent breast? That, more than stone, ne'er soft compassion mov'd, who from its father seis'd his much belov'd."

HANCOCK

Thank you.

(Crossing to stand before the jury)

This, gentlemen of the jury, is written from her experience. Phillis knows first-hand the slaver's lash and chains. She has experienced the cold darkened hold of the Middle Passage. Are not these an experience of the tyranny of man?

OLIVER

Your Honor, Mr. Hancock would have us all justify any traitorous words or deeds to a bad personal experience.

HANCOCK

Your Honor!

HUTCHINSON

Yes, Mr. Hancock.

HANCOCK

Our destiny as a nation is linked with the destiny of this child who stands before us!

OLIVER

I object. The use of the word child is designed to bring sympathy to the defendant.

JURY

(Moans)

HUTCHINSON

You may proceed, Mr. Hancock.

HANCOCK

Mr. Green, and gentlemen of the jury, if you were gifted with the powers of expression that she has demonstrated this day, would you not express those deepest emotions?

OLIVER

Mr. Green?

GREEN

I have no further questions, your Honor.

HUTCHINSON

You may return, then, to the jury box, Mr. Green. Does anyone else want to question the defendant? Hearing none, I now will allow the defendant to conclude with her own statement.

HANCOCK

(Turning to face Phillis)

I know that it has been a long morning for you and that you are tired. I know that your voice grows weak and your cough grows strong, but if you find the strength, you may make your own statement at this time.

PHILLIS

(Pausing, looking toward the jury)

God has implanted a principle, which we call love of freedom. It is impatient of oppression, and pants for deliverance; and by the leave of our modern Egyptians I will assert that the same principles live in us, the Negroes and Indians of Boston and America. How well the cry for liberty and the exercise of oppressive power over others agree, I humbly think does not require the penetration of a philosopher to determine.

JURY

(Murmurings and nodding of heads in assent)

HANCOCK

Your Honor, in light of her testimony and her weakening condition, I suggest that Miss Phillis be allowed to retire now.

HUTCHINSON

Mr. Oliver, are you ready to conclude?

OLIVER

With the defendant, your Honor, yes. But I would like to call one more witness.

The Wheatley family rises in unison, protesting the prolonging of the trial.

SUSANNA

Your Honor, can't you see the child is sick? This inquisition must end or I fear for the consequences.

HUTCHINSON

Proceed, Mr. Oliver.

OLIVER

I call Mr. Nathaniel Wheatley.

Nathaniel crosses from his chair behind the defendant's cage where Phillis stands to take the witness chair and be sworn. There is a sudden crescendo of shouts from outside on King's Street below.

OLIVER
Now, sir, please state your name.

NATHANIEL
Nathaniel Wheatley.

OLIVER
And what is your age?

NATHANIEL
I am twenty-eight years old.

OLIVER
Aside from your immediate family, who else has lived in the Wheatley household?

NATHANIEL
Over the years we have had a few domestic servants, and of course, for the last decade, Phillis.

OLIVER
Do you not consider her a domestic servant?

NATHANIEL
She is to us as a member of the family.

OLIVER
I see. So you became a part of the effort of teaching your family's household slave to read and write?

Nathaniel looks to Phillis, and beyond, to his parents.

NATHANIEL
Along with my sister, Mary, who was and remains her tutor, and my mother, we all became Phillis's tutors. And I must say we all have found it very rewarding.

OLIVER
Mr. Wheatley, do you know that in the colonies to the south — say, in the Carolinas — it is a criminal offense to teach a slave to read and write? Indeed, there are severe penalties for that.

NATHANIEL
Thank God, this is Boston and Massachusetts, and we do not have such laws.

JURY

(Some laughter, murmurs of approval, and nodding in assent)

Chauncy rises from the jury bench.

HUTCHINSON

I recognize the Reverend Chauncy.

CHAUNCY

We have all been called to freedom. It is through education that we free the mind.

JURY

(Murmurs of assent)

OLIVER

Remarkable.

Oliver crosses to counsel's table, retrieves the manuscript with a dramatic flourish, and then crosses to the witness.

OLIVER

Do you write poetry?

NATHANIEL

I have tried my hand at it, but I must confess I am not very good.

OLIVER

Not good enough to write the poems in this manuscript?

Oliver holds the manuscript before Nathaniel.

NATHANIEL

It is not my work. It is Phillis's work. I do not claim to have such poetic talents.

OLIVER

And which of the masters of our language is your favorite poet?

NATHANIEL

I would have to say that is Alexander Pope.

OLIVER

(Feigning surprise)

Your family seems extraordinarily enamored of Mr. Pope.

NATHANIEL

As is most of Boston and America, I daresay.

JURY

(Laughter)

OLIVER

Just answer the question. You need not elaborate with your views.

NATHANIEL

Yes, sir.

Oliver crosses back to Nathaniel and leans in close.

OLIVER

Do you consider yourself to be a loyal subject of King George the Third?

NATHANIEL

Yes, he is our King.

OLIVER

And as such, you would not do any act that would be against His Majesty's government here in the colony?

NATHANIEL

Act?

OLIVER

Any act — write a poem or an essay, work against certain institutions, sign a declaration attesting to being a terrorist?

NATHANIEL

Would I...

OLIVER

Let me rephrase the question. Have you ever engaged in any activity that was designed to undermine His Majesty's government? And let me caution you before you answer, that there are severe penalties for perjury, and you have taken an oath under God to tell the truth.

NATHANIEL

I am well aware of my oath.

Hancock rises from counsel's table.

HUTCHINSON

For what purpose does Mr. Hancock rise?

HANCOCK

Mr. Wheatley is not alone in his judgments on some edicts of Parliament that are autocratic and therefore have to be challenged.

Suddenly, there is a crescendo of huzzahs and shouts from outside. The courtroom falls silent momentarily. The doors of the Governor's Council Chamber Room burst open. A medium sized man dressed as a gentleman enters and crosses to stand before Hutchinson. The assembled sit in stunned silence.

HUTCHINSON

What is this intrusion? Who are you?

MACKINTOSH

It is the intrusion of the people, and
I am the people's true representative.
I am here, and outside my men have
surrounded this chamber. We are here
for you two: Hutchinson and Oliver. We
want you to come now and join us for
some sport on Pope's Day.

Mackintosh crosses to the French doors and stands there, raising his arms. There is a roar of voices from King's Street below. Mackintosh then crosses back to center stage.

OLIVER

It is Ebenezer Mackintosh.

MACKINTOSH

Speak up, old man. You whisper like an
old man who has lost his wits.

JURY

(Shouts in condemnation of Mackintosh)

ELLIOT

(Rising)

Be gone, you.

COOPER

(Rising, pointing)

Go! Go!

BYLES

To the perdition from which you came!

MACKINTOSH

Your words are hollow. I have the only army here. I have the people behind me. Did you not hear them? Need I go to the window again and summon my troops up here?

HUTCHINSON

(Pounding his gavel)

Order, order!

Hancock crosses to confront Mackintosh.

HANCOCK

You are wrong, sir! There is another set of troops assembled now at the Common, and upon my command I can have them here.

MACKINTOSH

Do you not fear a riot? A massacre?

HANCOCK

I do not refer to the British troops who occupy our city. I would not ask — even them — to remove the likes of you. It would be like me calling upon Satan to remove the invisible demon who accompanies you.

MACKINTOSH

Sir, your words smack of treason. And tell me, where is your army?

HANCOCK

I am the colonel of the Corps of Cadets. They have assembled at the Common, and await my order!

MACKINTOSH

American-born cadets?

HANCOCK

One thousand strong, at my command! As different from British troops as night from day.

HUTCHINSON

Mr. Hancock!

MACKINTOSH

You do indeed speak rebellion. I see no army.

Crossing to the French doors, Hancock opens them against the wind and cold, and steps onto the balcony. There is a huge roar of approval from below, even louder than the one for Mackintosh. Hancock steps back and crosses to face Mackintosh.

HANCOCK

You see, Mr. Mackintosh, I have many friends even in your army.

HUTCHINSON

(To Mackintosh)

I command you to leave. Mr. Hancock speaks the truth; he has my commission as colonel of the Corps of Cadets.

MACKINTOSH

(Raising his fist toward the bench)

Fie on you! We will get you!

Mackintosh exits.

HUTCHINSON

(Visibly relieved)

Now that he has departed, we must speedily conclude these proceedings. The danger of more interruptions remains strong.

HANCOCK

As you wish, your Honor. I believe that would be best for all at this time.

HUTCHINSON

Mr. Prosecutor, do you have a closing statement?

OLIVER

Your Honor, I need to cross-examine the witness Nathaniel Wheatley.

Oliver crosses to counsel's table, picks up the scroll, and returns to stand before the jury. He dramatically unfurls the scroll.

OLIVER

I hold in my hand—

HUTCHINSON

Mr. Prosecutor, this is not the time. Give me the scroll, please.

OLIVER

Your Honor, this is the evidence, the proof...

HUTCHINSON

But the time has passed.

Oliver is still standing, holding the scroll and facing the bench.

OLIVER

But, your Honor. The scroll.

HUTCHINSON

Mr. Oliver, do you have a closing statement?

Somewhat shaken and frustrated, Oliver hesitates momentarily, trying to reorganize his thoughts. The scroll falls to the floor where it furls back up.

OLIVER

Yes — yes, your Honor, and I will be brief.

(Crossing to stand before the jury)

Gentlemen of the jury, you are all successful men otherwise you would not be here. You have heard the testimony and now you must decide. Is Miss Phillis - a Negro slave just ten years removed from the wilds of Africa — the true and sole author of these poems? As you consider that question, think carefully on your own distinguished careers. Consider closely, if we all do sign our names, what might happen when that signed document is published? Once signed, there is no taking our names off of that list. It becomes the permanent record. It will become part of your legacy, Boston's legacy, this Province's legacy. Is this how you want to be remembered as one who signed an Attestation that could be a fraud. Can you afford to take that chance? We have heard evidence, but have we seen and heard proof? Is attesting to this slave's authorship of these poems worth risking your own legacies? For the Attestation will live on after you have passed. Let me conclude by reminding you that if any one of you still harbors doubts, you have an obligation to express them now for all of our reputations, as well as the reputation of this Town, this Province.

HUTCHINSON

Thank you, Mr. Oliver.

HANCOCK

If I may, your Honor, a few words in closing?

HUTCHINSON

Proceed.

Another great roar is heard from the streets below.

HANCOCK

As with you, gentlemen of the jury, I would never lend my name to a document or undertaking about which I harbored any doubts. Now we come to the moment of truth and we must ask ourselves a question: are we so molded from birth, upbringing, and education that we cannot conceive that a young woman native-born of Africa, brought to these shores less than a dozen years ago as a slave, could possibly do things that do not fit within our narrow concepts?

He gestures to where Phillis stands in the defendant's box.

HANCOCK

Indeed, that someone so born and brought hither could possibly do things better than we ourselves might be able to do. I for one am not a poet — as I know some of you in this room to be. Yet, I know in my heart the muse of all great and good poetry is truth. Nor do I doubt that Phillis — who stands before us — is the true and sole author of these poems.

OLIVER

Indeed, you speak for yourself.

HANCOCK

Mr. Oliver, I did not interrupt you during your closing statement. I would

appreciate it if you showed me the same
courtesy.

HUTCHINSON

Proceed, Mr. Hancock.

HANCOCK

Today we have been warned in a most offensive way about the possible repercussions from the mob if we do not stop this proceeding. But the achievements of this young girl who stands before us are not to be feared. They are to be welcomed. Gentlemen of the jury, how else could Phillis assert herself in this world but through her poetry? It is through this poetry that ultimately she declares her faith in God, her worth, her humanity in a hostile world.

Another loud crescendo of shouts is heard from the streets; the noise is growing in ferocity and anger.

HUTCHINSON

Mr. Hancock, I must remind you we need to conclude these proceedings before there is another interruption.

HANCOCK

Thank you, Your Honor, and let me conclude with one final observation.

Today we have been reminded by a slave girl how precious is our liberty. If she holds liberty as one of her most sacred values, what must our commitment to liberty be? She has reminded us that we must renew our commitment by all lawful ways and means in our power, that we will maintain, defend, and preserve those civil and religious rights and liberties so that we will be able to hand them down to future generations. That concludes my remarks.

HUTCHINSON

Thank you, Mr. Hancock. Members of the jury, as a matter of procedure, you see the attestation there upon the podium. Should you decide that the defendant is the true and sole author of these poems, I ask you to approach the podium individually and sign the attestation, and then you may leave. If you decide not to sign, you may leave directly.

All rise. The jurors stand as the governor steps down from the dais. The lieutenant governor follows him. The jury files toward the exit. John Hancock stands next to counsel's table looking toward Phillis. He bows his head somewhat wearily, and then slowly turns and crosses to the podium where the attestation rests. He takes the quill from the inkwell and signs his name. As the Wheatleys cross to Phillis, the jury files toward the podium in a line, with Joseph Green leading. Hutchinson and Oliver hesitate momentarily until all have signed. When there is no one at the podium, first Hutchinson, and then Oliver, approach to sign. The stage grows dark. Phillis is alone in the spotlight.

CURTAIN

Suggestions for Further Reading

Carretta, Vincent, Phillis Wheatley Complete Writings, edited with an introduction, Penguin Books, 2001.

Davis, David Brion, The *Problem of Slavery in the Age of Revolution 1770–1823.* 2nd ed. Oxford: Oxford University Press, 1999.

Fowler, William M. Jr., The Baron of Beacon Hill, Houghton Mifflin Company, Boston, 1980.

Gates, Henry Louis, The Trials of Phillis Wheatley: America's First Black Poet and Her Encounters with the Founding Fathers, 2003. Perseus Books, 2010, New York.

Hall, Kermit L., *The Magic Mirror: Law in American History*. 1989.

Hargrave, Francis, An *Argument in the Case of James Somerset a Negro,* London, 1774.

Higginbotham, A. Leon., *In the Matter of Color: Race and the American Legal Process, The Colonial Period. 1978.*

Labaree, Benjamin Woods, The Boston Tea Party, Northeastern University Press, Boston, 1964.

Richmond, Merle, American Women of Achievement, Phillis Wheatley Poet, Chelsea House Publishers, New York, Philadelphia, 1998.

Somerset v Stewart, Lofft 1–18; 20 Howell's State Trials 1, 79–82; 98 E.

Unger, Harlow Giles, American Tempest How the Boston Tea Party Sparked the Revolution, Publisher, Da Capo Press, 2012.

Zobel, Hiller B., The Boston Massacre, W, W, Norton, New York, 1970.

About the Author

A lawyer, Ronald Wheatley is a student of history and a member of the Massachusetts Society of the Sons of the American Revolution (MASSAR). He served as a Peace Corps Volunteer in Nigeria, West Africa in the mid-sixties. After his return to America he taught for a year in an inner city Junior High in Tacoma, Washington. He then was drafted into the U. S. Army and served with the 1st Signal Brigade in Vietnam from 1967-1968, He is married to Ethel Kent Wheatley originally from Brooklyn, New York. They have two grown children, John and Elizabeth, with the latter having designed the cover of both of his books. The author and his wife live in Scituate, Massachusetts. While he had traced his bloodline six generations to Wheatley family patriarch Leonard Wheatley of Virginia who served on the Continental line, he is now in the process of tracing his family back to the Wheatley's of Boston, but in any event, he considers himself a descendant of the Wheatley's of Boston if not by sanguinity, then by spirit.

Made in the USA
San Bernardino, CA
22 April 2017